BREAKING FREE

I am writing this book as a way to heal. It seems as though I have spent most of my time living in the past and hold on to how I feel about it. I don't usually share details of what I went through. When I finally feel ready to open up I never know what to say, where to start or who to share with. I am writing this as a way to let go and move on. I hope whoever is reading this can find the strength they need to heal as well. The names of everyone mentioned in this book have been changed in order to respect their privacy.

I am dedicating this book to my mom, dad, and cousins. Thank you for always believing in me, and pushing me to be the best, strongest version of myself.

PREFACE

Growing up, I had always been an inherently shy individual.
This aspect of my personality became evident during my early
years in school. I distinctly recall a moment in first grade when
my teacher, Mrs. Baker, called on me to count money that was
projected onto the whiteboard. I possessed the knowledge and
ability to accurately count coins, and I knew what the correct
answer was.. However, as soon as I heard my name uttered
from Mrs. Baker's mouth, an overwhelming sense of paralysis
washed over me. I found myself incapable of speaking, my
face reddened, and tears welled up in my eyes. It felt as though
I had forgotten how to breathe, my palms grew clammy, and
my heart raced with an unrelenting intensity. In that pivotal
moment, I remained silent long enough for Mrs. Baker to
redirect her attention to another student. This pattern of

freezing in anxious situations persisted throughout the majority of my school years.

The anxiety I experienced manifested itself prominently in various classroom scenarios. I vividly recall entering my third-grade classroom with a sense of dread, particularly when it came to the math portion of our lessons. Mathematics proved to be a personal struggle, and as luck would have it, I was frequently called upon to answer questions or solve problems. It appeared to many that I was not paying attention during class, as my gaze would often wander around the room. However, this outward behavior stemmed from a deep-seated anxiety rather than a lack of focus or interest.

The anxiety-induced freezing response extended beyond math class. I can still recall instances when I was called upon to read even a single sentence from a book. Once again, I would find myself in a state of mental and emotional paralysis. The words on the page seemed to blend together, resembling an unfinished puzzle, and my vision would momentarily fade into darkness. Summoning the strength to push through this overwhelming sensation, I would attempt to read aloud, only to find myself stuttering due to the rush of adrenaline coursing through my veins. Whether I read too slowly, attempting to grasp control over the words, or too quickly, desperately seeking an escape from the situation, both approaches inevitably resulted in stumbling over my words.

Despite the battle with anxiety that had begun at such a young age, I was, in essence, a typical child who delighted in boy bands, enjoyed expressing myself through art, and revealed in moments of lighthearted silliness.

~~~~

"We should walk all the way to Clough. Can't we get there if we just walk through your backyard?" asked Natalie, my then 16 year old cousin. Natalie was the oldest among us and had a knack for coming up with the most daring ideas.

"You're right. We should pack bags to bring with us on our trip," I replied, excitedly embracing the adventure that lay ahead.

As Natalie and I brainstormed a packing list, my cousin Eddie diverted his attention to his usual pursuit—searching for frogs. It had become a customary activity whenever they slept over at my house. Late at night or early in the morning, we would venture outside to catch frogs, carefully assigning names to our amphibious companions.

"Before we head on this trip, we should ask my mom for permission and see if we can bring Kaelyn along," I expressed, mindful of keeping my mom informed about my whereabouts and activities.

Earlier that day, my mom had left to pick up my younger cousin, Kaelyn, who was only six years old. Thankfully, my mom embraced the idea, granting us permission to proceed. We swiftly packed our bags, donned our trusty rain boots, and stocked up on sunscreen. And just like that, Natalie, Eddie, Kaelyn, and I set off on an exhilarating walk through the woods behind my house.

As we ventured deeper into the woods, my mom's voice rang out from the deck, cautioning us, "Follow the river so you don't get lost." Her advice reminded us of the meandering nature of rivers, which we had failed to consider. To reach Clough from my house, we would need to walk in a straight line, disregarding the river's twists and turns.

Just before we continued our journey, my mom whispered, "Oh, and uh, watch out for snakes." She specifically wanted to alert Natalie, knowing that out of all the children, I was the one most likely to become flustered at the sight of a snake.

As we traversed the woods, time seemed to slip away. Kaelyn busily collected acorns, while Natalie discovered a trove of baby tree frogs. Meanwhile, I captured our adventure on video, and Eddie diligently tracked our progress on his phone.

At a certain point, we stumbled upon what appeared to be a lumber yard. The discovery took us by surprise. How could this be? It was located right behind my house, and we had never noticed its existence before. The presence of orange spray-painted trees and scattered logs hinted at its purpose.

"Hey, there's somebody over there," Natalie alerted us, her voice tinged with curiosity and caution.

We found ourselves in uncharted territory, unsure of our exact location. I called my mom, who embarked on a virtual journey using Google Maps, attempting to determine where we were or where we might be. In the meantime, she advised us to continue walking, hoping we would stumble upon a familiar landmark. She stayed on the phone with us, and Eddie utilized his GPS to pinpoint our position.

"We're in Concord," Eddie announced, his words met with disbelief from my mom.

"What? There's no way you could have made it all the way to Concord," my mom exclaimed, her concern evident.

"But we've been walking for two hours," I replied, my voice laced with exhaustion and dehydration due to the scorching heat.

"It would take you longer than two hours to walk to Concord," my mom reassured us, her worry mounting.

Resolute, we forged ahead, heeding my mom's advice. She disconnected from Google Maps and decided to drive around, searching for any sign of our whereabouts. As we pressed onward, we encountered a steep hill. Reaching its summit, we paused, relishing a moment of tranquility that swiftly transformed into agitation.

"Look! A snake!" Eddie exclaimed with a mix of excitement and fear.

I screamed, catching a mere glimpse of the serpent's tail as it slithered into the tall grass that lay before us. Fearful and unnerved, I staunchly refused to proceed. At that moment, my mom instructed us to turn back and return to the lumber yard where we had earlier spotted another person. Perhaps they could provide us with directions or an address from a nearby mailbox.

Upon our return to the lumber yard, I whispered to my cousins, my voice tinged with concern, "What if this place is a slaughterhouse?" I made a conscious effort to keep my voice low, ensuring that Kaelyn wouldn't overhear. However, anyone familiar with my childhood self would know that I tended to be quite boisterous when I was with them.

Nervously, Kaelyn voiced her apprehension, saying, "I don't want to die today."

As we cautiously approached the house, we found no one in sight. Proceeding toward the road in search of a street sign, Eddie appeared momentarily perplexed, as if a sense of recognition washed over him.

"Wait, Annabelle, isn't this your road?" he asked, his tone filled with a mixture of surprise and realization.

I surveyed the surroundings for a brief moment and came to the startling realization that indeed, we had stumbled upon my road. Moments later, my mom's car pulled up behind us. She had managed to catch up with our wandering group. As we gratefully climbed into the car, we engaged in a simple exercise, counting the number of houses between our current location and mine. In a nutshell, it took us a staggering two hours to walk a mere four houses down.

This exhilarating adventure served as a reminder that even the most straightforward paths can lead to unexpected destinations. It underscored the importance of caution, preparedness, and a sense of direction in our endeavors. Above all, it solidified the notion that no matter how far we wander, the comfort and security of home always await our return.

ONE

Shattered Hearts

Every girl dreams of her first love. I remember being young and watching shows and movies on the Disney Channel, where first love was always portrayed as a magical experience filled with anticipation and hope. It seemed like a world where butterflies danced in your stomach and everything was perfect. However, the reality of first love is often far from these idealized portrayals. It can lead us down unexpected paths, where darkness lurks beneath the surface.

I was twelve years old when I started seventh grade, and my small town welcomed several new students. Most of them were nervous and shy, as one would expect, but there was one exception—Jack. He exuded an extraordinary level of extroversion and even had a hint of cockiness about him. In the first week of school, Jack had already asked out at least ten girls, on seven different occasions. Initially, most girls found him irritating and wanted nothing to do with his childish middle school games. Little did I know that my feelings towards him would soon change, along with those of many others.

Gradually, all the girls in our class began to fall for Jack's charm. It seemed as though anyone not with him was filled with envy, while simultaneously swooning over him. I, too, found myself falling for his allure. We started dating, and in the beginning, everything seemed perfect—until it wasn't. Within a week, his charming facade started to fade, revealing a darker side of his personality. He began playing jokes on me, but these were not the harmless kind of jokes that made others laugh. Instead, he would convince me that he was cheating on me or planning to break up. While some might dismiss these incidents as trivial due to the young age of our relationship. For me, someone with an anxious attachment style and anxiety in general, they were far from settling.

Coincidentally, it seemed as though Jack always chose meal times to play these mind games. I believe, to this day, that it was unintentional. During lunch, he would share these jokes with others, and inevitably, they would reach me. The anxiety of betrayal and impending heartbreak would overwhelm me, robbing me of my appetite no matter how hungry I had been just moments before. I could hardly bring myself to eat my lunch, maybe picking at a tater tot here or there, but never having a full meal. While the issues were resolved by the end of the school day, the torment would resume when I got home for dinner, as Jack would start the same destructive cycle through text messages. Once again, I would lose my appetite, and my dinner would go untouched.

Prior to this relationship, I was already someone who rarely ate breakfast. Perhaps it was due to the anticipation and anxiety of the day ahead. But when you add it all up, it meant that I wasn't eating at all. This detrimental pattern continued for about four months, until I finally gathered the strength to break up with him. By that point, I had become underweight, trapped in the grip of a destructive relationship that took a toll on both my emotional well-being and physical health.

~~~~

Mr. Clark was not just an ordinary teacher. To me, he was an unwavering source of support and guidance during my 7th-grade year. Little did I know that Mr. Clark's profound impact would extend far beyond the realm of the classroom.

From the moment he learned about my anxiety, Mr. Clark became my steadfast ally, a pillar of strength amid the loud storm that raged within me. His dedication to helping me navigate the labyrinth corridors of anxiety was inspiring. He possessed an innate ability to discern the silent battles that waged behind my anxious facade, and his empathetic nature allowed him to approach my struggles with unwavering compassion.

Understanding the debilitating nature of anxiety, Mr. Clark embarked on a mission to provide me with the tools I needed to confront and overcome my inner demons. He tailored his teaching methods to create a safe and nurturing environment where I could freely express my concerns and fears. Classroom discussions became opportunities for me to confront my anxieties head-on, as Mr. Clark skillfully guided me through the maze of my racing thoughts, helping me gain a sense of control over the chaos that threatened to engulf me.

In moments of overwhelming panic, Mr. Clark's calm presence served as an anchor, grounding me in the reality that I was not alone in my struggle. He encouraged me to confide in him, assuring me that my feelings were valid and deserving of attention. He taught me the power of self-compassion, urging me to acknowledge that setbacks were a natural part of the journey towards growth. He reminded me that anxiety did not define me, but rather it was a facet of my being that could be tamed through perseverance and self-belief. If I hadn't reached out to him about what I was going through, he would not have helped me in the ways that he did. Make a note that reaching out can be a very positive attribute.

~~~~

During the period when Jack and I were apart, I had my annual doctor's appointment. It was during this visit that my doctor expressed her concern about my behavior and warned me about the potential development of an eating disorder if I continued down this path. Taking her advice seriously, she referred me to a nutritionist, and for a while, it seemed like things were improving. However, despite my efforts, I began to notice the numbers on the scale creeping up once again.

~~~~

Throughout my entire life, certain family members had always felt the need to comment on my appearance and weight. Whether it was directly to my face, poking fun at me, or criticizing my parents. These remarks seemed to find their way into every family gathering. One particular occasion that stands out is the annual Valentine's Day party at my Nona's house. My cousins and I would gather to decorate cupcakes and cookies with frosting and sprinkles. My parents, understanding my young and innocent cravings, allowed me to enjoy these treats whenever I wanted. This permissive approach actually helped me develop a healthy relationship with food. I never felt the need to overeat or hide food, as I learned that I could have sweets or chips whenever the desire struck. However, even the simplest act of licking a small amount of frosting off my finger would trigger my Aunt Tyra and Uncle Roy to make snide comments to my parents. The weight of their words would burrow deep into my impressionable mind.

One person I always enjoyed spending time with was my cousin Natalie. As an only child, I looked up to her as an older sister. On one occasion, I spontaneously went to her house, eager to go swimming in her pool. However, I had forgotten to bring a bathing suit, so she generously lent me one of her bikinis. As a seven-year-old, this made me feel grown up and excited. But my aunt, Taryn, who joined us for the swim, couldn't resist pointing out the size of my stomach and giggling about it. Inevitably, these comments fueled my hyperfocus on my appearance and exacerbated the insecurities that were already taking root within me.

~~~~

I didn't regain all the weight I had previously lost, but enough for me to notice the changes in my body. Insecurity started to take hold, and I found myself consistently donning the same oversized hoodie and leggings, using them as a shield to hide my self-perceived flaws. As the 8th grade began, I entered into a relationship with Jack once again.

Attending middle school dances was a regular occurrence for Jack and I. Our routine usually involved him riding my bus to my house, where my mom would then drive us to the school for the dance. Afterward, his mom would kindly drop me back home. However, on one particular evening, Jack's mom, who worked at the school, had to stay a bit longer to assist with the post-dance cleanup. Seizing the opportunity to spend more time together, Jack and I ventured outside to join our friends who were being picked up by their parents.

As the night progressed, the air grew colder. The atmosphere was still and quiet, with a hint of excitement lingering from the dance. With each passing minute, the number of departing friends increased until we found ourselves alone outside. Seeking warmth and comfort in each other's presence, Jack pulled me into a tight hug. Then, as I gazed up at him, our eyes locked, and a profound silence enveloped us. In that moment, he leaned in and pressed his lips against mine. It was an electrifying sensation, my first kiss—a gentle and delicate exchange of affection that carried with it a multitude of emotions. Initially, everything seemed wonderful, but it was during the summer before high school that the tides began to turn.

It felt as though we were constantly at odds with each other. Every disagreement, every issue, was swiftly labeled as "my fault," leaving me in a state of perpetual apprehension. Already struggling with effective communication, this situation exacerbated my difficulties, making me even worse at expressing myself. Despite my efforts to communicate my feelings and establish boundaries, Jack possessed a remarkable ability to manipulate any situation to his advantage, skillfully flipping it around to portray himself as the victim.

His manipulation tactic further distorted my perception of reality and made it increasingly challenging to assert my needs and concerns. I often felt trapped and suffocated within the confines of the relationship, always second-guessing myself and living in fear of his emotional outbursts. The power dynamics were imbalanced, and I became more and more isolated from my own voice and agency.

Abuse is a cycle. And since this book explains the concepts of these types of relationships quite numerously, it is important to understand how these cycles function. The cycle consists of four steps. The first one being referred to as the "calm". This is when everything seems perfect. Oftentimes, the abuser will "love bomb". Meaning they will give you gifts, affection and endless compliments. Next, "tension builds". There becomes a lack of communication and the victim becomes fearful. Then there is the "incident". This is when any type of abuse occurs, whether it be emotional, physical, verbal or sexual. And lastly, "reconciliation". The abuser may apologize, but will quickly turn the situation around on the victim. Shifting the blame to them. They may also deny the abuse ever happened. These four steps of the cycle can last for any amount of time. Always making its way back to the "calm" phase.

TWO

Watering a Dead Flower

Throughout all of my struggles, there was one constant in my
life—a required art class that became a refuge for my battered
soul. Despite the turmoil I faced, the art class sparked a
glimmer of excitement within me. But as I walked into that
classroom, tears streaming down my face, the weight of the
day's abuse from Jack still fresh, I found solace in the presence
of a remarkable classmate—Eden.

Eden possessed an extraordinary wisdom beyond her
years and an awe-inspiring talent for art. I marveled at her

creations, astounded by her ability to bring life to the canvas. Amidst my frequent breakdowns, she never turned away or dismissed my tears. Instead, she showed genuine curiosity, urging me to share the source of my pain. In those vulnerable moments, Eden became not only a compassionate listener but also a source of invaluable guidance.

I recall one particular conversation with Eden that has remained etched in my memory. As I poured my heart out to her, explaining the constant effort I was putting into a failing relationship, she offered me a metaphor that would forever transform my perspective. With unwavering compassion, she spoke these words: "Annabelle, you are watering a dead flower. No matter how much water or love you give this relationship, it's not going to change; it's dead."

Eden's profound insight resonated deeply within me. Her words carried a universal truth—one that extended beyond my specific situation. That simple yet poignant quote became a beacon of clarity, reminding me that sometimes, despite our best efforts and intentions, certain relationships and circumstances are beyond saving. It served as a reminder that investing time, energy, and love in something that cannot thrive or grow only depletes our own well-being.

But beyond the relationship context, Eden's advice held a much broader significance. It spoke directly to the core of my being, urging me to recognize my worth and prioritize self-care. In those transformative words, she reminded me that while relationships may wither, and circumstances may crumble, I, as an individual, am not a dead plant. I am deserving of nurturing, care, and love. It was a call to redirect my focus, to shift my attention towards my own growth, healing, and self-discovery.

And so, dear reader, as you continue your journey through life, I implore you to hold onto Eden's wisdom. Remember that you, too, are not a dead plant. Regardless of the trials you face, the pain you endure, or the relationships that falter, you possess an innate resilience and a wellspring of potential within you. Embrace the art of self-care, pour love and attention onto yourself, and nurture the seeds of your own growth.

THREE

Survivor

The continuous cycle of arguments and manipulation took a
toll on my emotional well-being and self-esteem. The constant
blame and shifting of responsibility chipped away at my sense
of self-worth, leaving me feeling inadequate and undeserving
of love and respect. It became a struggle to find my own voice
amidst the racket of Jack's persuasive tactics. I remember one
time we were FaceTiming and he had said,

"Annabelle, you're such a fucking idiot."

To some, the statement may seem minor, but for someone as sensitive as myself, those words cut deep. I internalized every insult, every derogatory term, and carried the weight of them in my heart. The emotional abuse within our relationship never ceased. I was constantly subjected to name-calling, being labeled a "bitch" or a "cunt." Whenever things didn't go his way, he would resort to threatening self-harm, leaving me in a state of panic and uncertainty. He would proceed to then not answer my texts or calls for hours on end. The anxiety of what he might do or had already done consumed me, continuing his control over me.

But there's one aspect of my experience that summer and throughout half of my freshman year that remains the hardest to let go of. It was during one of Jack's routine visits to my house. I had never been to his house due to my own anxieties and an uncomfortable feeling about his father. On this particular day, we found ourselves in the "hangout room," a cozy space with a few chairs and a television where we would spend time playing games or simply hanging out.

Engrossed in a game of Wii Sports, the atmosphere suddenly shifted. Out of nowhere, he placed his hand over my pants. Shock and confusion overcame me. At 14 years old, I had never really thought about sex or anything that came with it. He began to rub his hand over my pants, and I stood there in a state of utter disbelief. I was frozen, unsure of how to react or what to say. After all, my mom was in the other room, seated at the counter. Over time, instances like these became a recurring theme in our relationship.

This violation of my boundaries and personal space left me emotionally scarred. I grappled with a profound sense of confusion, shame, and powerlessness. The weight of my silence and inability to speak up in that moment haunted me

As we entered our freshman year of high school, the situation took a turn for the worse. Jack's friendship with older students, juniors, and seniors, seemed to intensify the toxicity of our relationship. We had become the couple that spent every weekend together, but his demands and threats became increasingly relentless. He would manipulate me by threatening not to come over unless I complied with his requests, gradually eroding my boundaries week after week.

I struggled to discern whether this behavior should be classified as grooming or manipulation, but regardless, he continued to assault me. He would coax me into allowing him to touch me, starting above my underwear, and eventually progressing to touching me beneath it. The same pattern persisted when he wanted me to touch him.

Throughout it all, I was never comfortable with any of these actions. I was neither ready nor willing to give that part of myself to someone who didn't treat me with the respect and care I deserved. However, summoning the courage to say "no" proved difficult, as he resorted to physical violence whenever I defied his demands. There were instances where he even hit me at school in front of teachers, yet no action was taken. To my dismay, he would even take out his anger on my dog, Sully, when he became sufficiently enraged.

He possessed a charm that made everyone believe he was merely joking, adding to my own confusion and self-doubt. For instance, when we walked alone in the hallway and I happened to share something that brought me joy, he would abruptly slam me against the lockers. His face would contort into an expression of pure malevolence, only to swiftly transition into a smile, as if to signal that it was all just a "joke."

~~~~

My math teacher, Mr. Wade, offered support. With keen observation, he noticed the distress caused by Jack's actions and attempted to intervene. In an effort to mitigate the harm, he made the decision to separate us in class. Unfortunately, this measure alone did not completely shield me from Jack's venom. During exams, Jack would unleash a downpour of screams and profanities in front of the entire class, directing them at me. The weight of his verbal assault left me feeling humiliated, hurt, and helpless. As tears streamed down my face, I couldn't escape the acute awareness that my classmates bore witness to this ugly spectacle. Math exams, already a source of anxiety, became excruciatingly overwhelming in the face of such public humiliation.

However, Mr. Wade did not turn a blind eye. Despite his limited power to control Jack's behavior, he made genuine efforts to provide support. Sensing my pain, he would approach with boxes of tissues, silently acknowledging the emotional toll the abuse exacted on me. He would gently remind me that there was hope beyond the confines of this abusive relationship.

"4 + 4 will still equal 8," he would softly affirm, using the language of mathematics as a metaphor for the consistency and predictability that existed beyond the chaos of my current situation.

In those simple words, he sought to reassure me that the abuse I faced was not a variable in my life equation. It wouldn't alter the fundamental truths or diminish my worth. With every gentle reminder, he urged me to consider a future free from the grip of Jack's abuse, a future where I could reclaim my peace of mind and well-being.

~~~~

Comparisons to other girls were another weapon in Jack's arsenal. In his presence, he would openly discuss what he found attractive in other girls, emphasizing their physical attributes, while I stood by as if invisible. I was never "skinny enough" or "curvy enough" for him. He insisted that I needed to "work out" or even consider undergoing plastic surgery to meet his standards. I constantly felt inadequate, striving for an unattainable version of myself that could satisfy his ever-shifting expectations.

Attending homecoming together was a milestone for me—my first high school dance. The excitement leading up to the night was palpable, as anticipation mingled with nervous energy. I had chosen a last-minute dress, a black ensemble that held a touch of whimsy and elegance. The top shimmered with delicate glitter, seamlessly transitioning into a short, flowy satin skirt that swirled with each step.

However, upon arriving at the school, a wave of self-doubt washed over me. As I observed the other girls, their figures accentuated by form-fitting dresses that seemed to command attention, a seed of insecurity took root within me. I found myself questioning my choice, suddenly feeling out of place amidst the sea of confident young women.

As the night unfolded, my initial excitement gradually morphed into a sense of loneliness. Jack seemed distant and preoccupied. Instead of spending time with me, he appeared to drift away, disappearing into the crowd of dancing couples. Every time I caught a glimpse of him, he was engrossed in the company of other girls on the dance floor and laughing, as if I were mere background noise.

The insecurity I had initially felt about my dress soon paled in comparison to the growing feelings of rejection and abandonment. Each time Jack left my side, my heart sank a little deeper. The distance between us seemed to widen, leaving me feeling isolated and invisible amidst the vibrant atmosphere of the dance.

The evening that was meant to be filled with joy, laughter, and shared moments turned into a series of fleeting encounters, brief glimpses of a connection that was slipping away. The hopes and expectations I had carried into the night crumbled, replaced by a cascade of tears that welled up, a tangible manifestation of my disappointment and heartache.

Little did I know, my first highschool dance, and my last would both end in tears, but we will get to that later.

As Halloween approached, an eagerness stirred within me to venture into the realm of haunted houses. While I had previously experienced ScreamFest at Canobie Lake Park, its scares failed to leave a lasting impression on me. Even with the comforting presence of light-up necklaces. This year, however, I yearned for a new and more exhilarating fright fest—Nightmare New England. The prospect of stepping into the unknown without my trusty glowing accessory made my nerves tingle, but I resolved to embrace the challenge.

My cousins Natalie, Ethan, and Eddie, along with their two friends and Eddie's then-girlfriend, had already formed a group to embark on this haunted adventure. Examining the headcount, I realized I would be left to navigate the spine-chilling attractions alone. I ended up inviting Jack to come with us. Yet, my decision caused annoyance among Natalie and Ethan. Their discomfort with Jack stemmed from his peculiar behavior in their presence. In awkward moments, he would direct unsettling comments towards Ethan, using names like "daddy" or "baby." Winking or playing footsie with him under the table during family dinners only added to the discomfort shared by everyone involved.

As we arrived at Nightmare New England, a mixture of anticipation and apprehension swirled within me. The absence of my familiar light-up necklace left me feeling vulnerable, unsure of how I would fare in the face of looming terrors. Little did I know that attempting to flee from the actors would only intensify the scares. They reveled in the pursuit, chasing those who dared to run. It was a valuable lesson—stand your ground and face the frights head-on.

The first haunted house we ventured into carried a clown theme. Though not overly terrifying, it seemed tailored to cater to a younger audience. Soon after, we embarked on the hayride—a personal favorite of mine. Here, the actors had the freedom to leap onto the hay-filled cart, their chilling touches amplifying the thrill of the experience.

Our journey continued through two more houses, each one pushing the boundaries of fear. As we reached the line for the final attraction, a sudden turn of events unfolded. My suspicions about Jack's vaping habits had lingered, even though he never openly admitted to it. Whenever I confronted him, he would vehemently deny any involvement, despite whispers from his friends affirming my doubts. I never had a problem with the idea of him vaping, since most of my friends also did. My main issue was the fact that he would lie to me about it.

To my astonishment, I witnessed Jack brazenly approaching Natalie and Ethan's friends, asking for a hit from their vape. I couldn't deny the truth before my eyes. Yet, when I confronted him once more, his practiced skill of gaslighting came into play. He looked me in the eye and denied his actions, effortlessly manipulating my trust. It was as if his words held a bewitching power, weaving a deceptive spell that clouded my judgment, momentarily casting doubt on what I knew to be true.

In that moment, a mixture of disappointment, confusion, and realization flooded over me. I had fallen victim to the art of manipulation, blinded by the desire to believe his words over the evidence before me. It was a reminder that appearances can be deceiving, and sometimes the scariest things lurk within the people we think we know best.

Throughout this nearly two-year cycle of abuse, I kept a journal as a means of capturing my emotions and experiences. In fact, I still have an entry from a month before we finally broke up, wherein I painstakingly detailed how I felt at that time.

I'm not okay. And I'm tired of pretending that I am. I'm tired of people telling me everything will be okay when I know it won't be. I'm tired of people saying "we'll fix this" when I know nothing will change. I'm so tired of false hope. I'm so tired of being sad. I miss the girl I was 6 months ago. I was always smiling and now I'm always crying. All because of somebody toxic that I don't want to lose. I don't know if I think anything will change. I don't know anything anymore. I'm physically and emotionally drained. Some may say I'm watering a dead plant and you know what, I guess I am. I don't know what I'm more scared of, being alone, or losing him. I guess I think that either way, with or without him I'll be sad. And maybe that's true. But it's whatever. I don't even think he cares about me anymore. Who would. Whenever I finally try to tell him how I feel, and how sad I am, and how sometimes I feel like the world would be better off without me, he just yells at me and threatens to tell my mom. But suddenly a new girl comes into the picture who made an awful mistake, and wants to kill herself too, and he stopped hanging out with me to go hang out with her to talk her out of it and make her feel better. And I can't even talk to him about this and how I feel, cause guess what… he'll just get mad at me. Maybe we're just not meant to be. Maybe he'll be happier without me. Is that what I want? Is that what I deserve? Is it okay? Should he get annoyed when I say no to certain topics? It's my body and my choice. I have the right to say no. It's not okay for him to tell me I'm bad at what I love. And it's not okay for him to tell me to stop talking when I'm excited about the things I love. It's not the same as it was 6 months ago. I've changed physically and mentally. He also changed. He got disrespectful. When I first started dating him I was a mess, then I was happy and confident. But I guess nothing really changed, cause I'm back where I started.

~~~~

I encourage those reading this to keep a journal, or even entries in the notes app of your phone. Oftentimes, it is hard to gather our thoughts when in these situations. It helps to minimize the overwhelmingness. It is also good to look back on months or even years down the line to see how much we have improved and grown.

When Jack and I reached the breaking point and finally ended our relationship midway through my freshman year, a glimmer of hope flickered within me. I naively believed that the turmoil I had endured would now fade into the past, and a sense of relief would wash over me. However, unbeknownst to me, the ordeal I had faced with Jack was merely the prelude to an even greater storm that awaited me.

After being with Jack, I couldn't help but feel guilty for being me. I felt shame for allowing myself to be treated so poorly. When you are young, your mind is very naive to relationships and everything that comes with it. You shouldn't blame yourself. You didn't know any better. It's so easy to be blinded by love. I thought being away from him would be the worst case scenario. But it was actually the best possible situation. Being out of the relationship, it was like the curtains were finally open. I finally saw how abusive and unhealthy our relationship was. My rose colored glasses were finally gone. I encourage you to leave your toxic relationships, it may seem impossible but in time, it will all be worth it.

FOUR

Putting Down the Pom-Poms

From the time I was in the fourth grade, cheerleading had been an integral part of my life. The joy and excitement of being part of a spirited team, the thrill of performing complex stunts, and the sense of closeness that came with it all were experiences I cherished. As I approached high school, I had every intention of continuing my cheerleading journey, despite the apprehensions that loomed over me.

Throughout my cheerleading career, I had primarily served as a backspot, leveraging my agility and strength to support my teammates during stunts. Despite my short stature, I had developed a knack for this position, finding comfort in my role as the anchor of the pyramid. However, with the transition to high school cheerleading, I knew I would be expected to step out of my comfort zone and embrace the position of a flyer. This prospect filled me with a mixture of excitement and fright. While I admired the grace and poise exhibited by the flyers, I also grappled with a nagging sense of doubt. Would my bases be able to support me? Could I trust them to catch me if I were to fall? The fear of injury and the potential for disappointment plagued my thoughts.

As a flyer, I had my fair share of tumbles and mishaps. My anxious tendencies and tense muscles often helped my stability in the air. While I excelled at certain stunts, the inconsistencies of my bases added an element of unpredictability to my performances. There were moments when my confidence wavered, as I found myself unceremoniously dropped on my face. The bruises and occasional embarrassment became a testament to the trials and tribulations inherent in the sport. Nevertheless, my love for cheerleading persevered.

Competitions held a special allure for me. Stepping onto the mat, surrounded by the fervent cheers of the crowd, and performing intricate routines in front of discerning judges, was an adrenaline rush like no other. The pressure was palpable, but I thrived in those moments, fueled by the electric atmosphere and the knowledge that my hard work and dedication were about to be put to the test. Pre-high school cheerleading had been a sanctuary of sorts, a realm devoid of drama where my teammates had become my family. However, the transition to high school brought with it a stark contrast. Drama seemed to permeate the team, casting a shadow over the otherwise vibrant spirit of the sport. And at the center of it all was Jack, who had an uncanny knack for dating almost every girl on the team.

As his relationships with my teammates unfolded, so did the complications. The intermingling of personal lives and romantic entanglements introduced an unsettling dynamic within the team, one that overshadowed the joy and unity I had previously associated with cheerleading. To make matters more complicated, Jack's sister was also a member of the cheer team. In the wake of our tumultuous breakup, I had counted on her understanding and support. We had shared a closeness that extended beyond our bond as teammates. But as the dust settled, she distanced herself from me, denying the validity of my experiences and the mistreatment I had endured. The loss of her friendship was a painful blow, adding to the weight of disappointment that had settled upon my cheerleading aspirations.

In the aftermath of those trying circumstances, I made the difficult decision to step away from cheerleading. The once vibrant and joyous activity had become marred by the toxicity and drama that had infiltrated my team. While I missed the thrill of performing, the connection with my teammates, and the sense of belonging, I found solace in knowing that I had preserved the memories

I empathize deeply with the arduous journey of relinquishing the things we hold dear. It is a path strewn with heartache and uncertainty, as we confront the agonizing realization that the very objects of our affection have transformed into agents of toxicity. Whether it be a cherished hobby, a person, a job, or any other aspect of our lives, the act of letting go becomes an imperative when they no longer nourish our souls or bring us the happiness we deserve.

Imagine, if you will, a garden suffused with vibrant blossoms, their fragrant petals enticing all who encounter them. These blossoms, once a source of profound joy and fulfillment, have now withered and wilted, their beauty tainted by a hidden poison. As we gaze upon this garden, tears well in our eyes, for we know that despite our love for these flowers, it is time to bid them farewell.

Walking away from something we once loved is a formidable feat, for it requires us to confront the stark reality that our emotional well-being is at stake. The tendrils of familiarity and comfort wrap tightly around our hearts, whispering seductive promises of nostalgia and familiarity. We find ourselves torn, grappling with conflicting emotions as we wrestle with the choice that lies before us.

In the grand tapestry of life, you deserve to flourish and thrive, surrounded by elements that elevate your spirit and ignite a fire within your soul. Just as the caterpillar emerges from its cocoon, undergoing a transformative metamorphosis, so too must you shed the burdens that hinder your growth.

FIVE

Starving for Control

Although I had severed ties with Jack, it felt as though his presence still loomed over my life, his influence seeping into every corner of my existence. While he effortlessly moved on, cycling through new girlfriends with alarming frequency, I was left grappling with the aftermath he had left me. This chapter of my life was not about him; it was about the wreckage I was left to navigate and repair on my own.

Even after our breakup, my relationship with food remained deeply troubled, and the repercussions were taking a toll on my physical and mental well-being. I found myself rapidly losing weight, trapped in the clutches of an insidious battle with body dysmorphia. Every time I glanced in the mirror, I saw a distorted image of myself, perceiving an exaggerated version of my size and shape, despite the reality of my severe underweight condition. The mirror became both a source of obsession and self-flagellation as I spent countless hours scrutinizing every inch of my body, evaluating my worthiness based on its appearance. A never-ending cycle of self-criticism and self-denial consumed my thoughts, leaving me trapped in a relentless pursuit of an unattainable ideal.

My struggles with body dysmorphia were not the only demons I faced. The trauma inflicted by Jack had taken its toll, leaving me with post-traumatic stress disorder (PTSD). Nightmares plagued my sleep, and flashbacks of the abuse I endured haunted my waking moments. The constant presence of Jack at school only served to intensify these distressing reminders. While I had the opportunity to report him for the sexual assault I experienced, my mother, with her well-intentioned concern for my well-being, discouraged me from pressing charges. She recognized the added stress and trauma that would accompany legal proceedings and believed that sparing me that burden was the best course of action.

It was during my annual appointment with my doctor that the extent of my struggles became officially recognized.

She confirmed my self-diagnosis of an eating disorder. Understanding the urgency of my situation, she referred me to a specialized treatment center where I could embark on the challenging journey of recovery.

The prospect of seeking professional help was daunting yet necessary. It offered a glimmer of hope, a lifeline to reclaim my life from the clutches of trauma and disordered eating. With the support of medical professionals and therapeutic interventions, I hoped to rebuild my shattered self-image, confront the demons of my past, and forge a path towards healing and self-acceptance. Although the road ahead seemed laborious, I clung to the belief that with the right guidance and a fierce determination to overcome, I could emerge from this darkness and reclaim my identity beyond the confines of my painful past.

The treatment center became a pivotal chapter in my journey towards recovery, although it presented its own set of challenges and disappointments. From the onset, it became evident that their focus was not on the well-being and healing of their patients but instead on maximizing their financial gains. This realization left a bitter taste in my mouth, highlighting the inherent flaws in the healthcare system that prioritized profit over genuine care.

My first day at the center was dedicated to intake procedures. It involved meetings with interns, nurses, and psychologists, all aimed at gaining a deeper understanding of my psychological state and determining the most appropriate course of treatment. It was during this process that they officially diagnosed me with Anorexia Nervosa, forever etching that label into my identity. The moment I received the diagnosis, an indescribable feeling washed over me. It was as if time stood still, and the world around me fell into a haunting silence. The weight of the diagnosis settled upon my shoulders, simultaneously validating my struggles and igniting a sense of fear for the difficult road that lay ahead.

The treatment center placed me in the Intensive Outpatient Program (IOP), which demanded my presence from Monday to Thursday, between the hours of 4 pm and 7 pm. However, the interns cautioned me that if my progress stagnated or deteriorated, they would consider transferring me to an inpatient program. This prospect filled me with dread. The thought of attending treatment for an extensive 10 hours a day, five days a week, coupled with the necessity of online schooling, loomed over me like an ominous cloud. The potential consequences of such a transition haunted my mind—how it would impact my chances of getting into future colleges and my ability to maintain social connections. It seemed that being removed from the everyday rhythm of life would only exacerbate my struggles, amplifying the sense of isolation and further impeding my path to recovery. With these concerns in mind, I resolved to give my utmost effort to the outpatient program, desperately hoping it would suffice to regain control over my life.

After my intake appointment at the treatment center, my mom and I decided to visit the mall. However, the joy I used to find in shopping for clothes had dwindled, replaced by a constant sense of frustration and self-comparison. Walking into stores became an exercise in disappointment, as I believed nothing would look good on me and my gaze would inevitably shift to the other girls browsing the racks. Despite my internal struggles, we ended up having lunch at Bertucci's, my favorite restaurant. Fettuccine Alfredo, my go-to meal, was a familiar comfort amidst the turbulent emotions and new diagnosis I was grappling with. During our meal, my mom and I delved into a conversation about anorexia, and she expressed her prior misconceptions about the disorder. I took the opportunity to explain the complexities and the various characteristics that accompanied it, helping her gain a deeper understanding. In that moment, the pieces of the puzzle started to come together, offering a glimmer of clarity amid the chaos.

The structure of the Intensive Outpatient Program (IOP) followed a carefully curated schedule, designed to facilitate healing and foster a sense of community among participants. The group therapy sessions, held from 4:00 to 5:00 pm, allowed us to share our experiences and provide support to one another. Most of the time, the interns would lead discussions on crucial topics like setting boundaries and cultivating resilience, equipping us with essential tools for our journey to recovery.

From 5:00 to 5:30 pm, our attention shifted towards dinner preparations. During this time, we were closely monitored to ensure no food was hidden or discarded. The watchful eyes of the staff reinforced the importance of completing our meals and confronting the anxieties surrounding food. At 5:30 pm, we gathered around the table to eat dinner together, again surveillanced by the presence of the interns who ensured we followed through with our meal plans. For those who struggled to finish their meals, leaving the room was not an option; instead, they were required to consume an

Ensure supplement. I took pride in my ability to consistently finish my meals, finding solace in the small victories along the way. However, there was one instance when I felt overwhelmed by nausea and an inability to keep any food down, leaving me perplexed as to why my body seemed to rebel against me.

After dinner, from 6:00 to 6:30 pm, we tidied up and returned to the same room where we had our group therapy sessions. This time, we engaged in a meditation practice that lasted approximately 10 minutes. On one occasion, instead of the usual guided meditation led by one of the interns, a recorded version played. To my surprise, the voice on the recording took on an eerie, almost demonic tone that struck me as comical. Unable to contain my laughter, it erupted uncontrollably, infecting those around me with a sense of shared amusement. However, the intern leading the session appeared annoyed by my outburst, despite the commonly held belief that laughter can be a powerful form of therapy and release.

The highlight of the IOP experience, from 6:30 to 7:00 pm, was the art therapy segment. It provided a welcome respite from the intensity of therapy and allowed us to express ourselves creatively. Engaging in various projects, such as making slime or glitter jars, offered a sense of playfulness and diversion from the weighty emotions we grappled with daily. These moments of artistic expression nurtured a spark of joy within me, reminding me that even amidst the darkness, there were glimpses of light and moments of respite.

In addition to attending the Intensive Outpatient Program (IOP), my treatment at the center also involved weekly meetings with a nurse and a family therapist. Unfortunately, the experiences with both professionals left much to be desired. Francesca, the nurse assigned to my case, delivered grim news about the fragility of my bones and how my body was cannibalizing its own muscle for energy. However, despite my mom and I repeatedly asking for guidance on what steps I needed to take to improve my condition, Francesca offered no concrete advice or explanations. The lack of guidance and support from someone who was supposed to be an integral part of my healing journey only added to the frustration and confusion.

The family therapist, Monica, proved to be equally disheartening. In our very first session, she shattered any semblance of hope by informing me that my chances of recovery were alarmingly low, citing a statistic that only 5% of people ever overcome their eating disorders. Instead of fostering a positive and empowering environment, Monica's negative demeanor further eroded my already fragile sense of self. Her discouraging words and lack of optimism clashed with her role as a therapist, whose primary duty should have been to instill hope and provide the necessary tools for recovery.

As I voiced my concerns about Monica's negativity, particularly in front of my dad, since he didn't attend the meetings with my mom and I. Despite sharing physical similarities with my mom, it is my dad with whom I have an uncanny resemblance when it comes to personality. We both possess an introverted nature and harbor a tendency toward anxiety. As if by some unspoken bond, my dad has an innate understanding of what goes on in the depths of my mind.

What sets my dad apart is his remarkable ability to comprehend the intricacies of my anxious mind. He recognizes the nuances of my concerns, sometimes even before I manage to articulate them myself. Whether it be a simple glance, a subtle change in my tone, or a pause in my speech, he has a way of deciphering the unspoken language of my anxiety.

My dad initially found it hard to believe that a therapist could be so detrimental to the healing process. However, his perspective shifted when he attended one of the meetings himself. He witnessed firsthand the discouraging statements and the lack of understanding on Monica's part. Her insistence on having others comment on my eating habits and her disregard for the coping mechanisms I had developed, such as watching shows or movies during meals, only fueled my frustration. For me, distraction provided a respite from the constant thoughts of restriction, yet Monica dismissed it as counterproductive. These interactions reinforced my growing belief that the treatment center's priorities were skewed, prioritizing profit over genuine concern for patients' well-being.

During this tumultuous period, my personality had become overshadowed by the eating disorder, which I often referred to as ED. ED dictated my actions and emotions, leading to outbursts of anger directed at my mom and moments of isolation where I refused to engage with the treatment process. The idea of attending IOP became an unbearable burden, leading to tears and desperate attempts to negotiate my way out of it through bribery, promising to indulge in certain foods if I was allowed to skip the sessions.

"If I don't go, I will eat TWO lobster rolls from D'Angelo's." I would say.

Although the treatment center was far from what I expected, my experience took an unexpected turn when I encountered a remarkable individual named Finn. From the moment I met him, it was evident that he possessed an extraordinary level of compassion towards everyone in the program. Initially, Finn had worked at a rehabilitation center dedicated to assisting individuals struggling with addiction. However, he approached eating disorders with the same heartfelt understanding and empathy. He also approached dealing with them in a similar way.

One particular evening during the Intensive Outpatient Program (IOP), Finn bestowed upon me one of the most incredible compliments I have ever received in my life. With genuine warmth in his eyes, he simply said, "You look so much happier." Those few words had a profound impact on me, resonating deeply within my soul. It was as if he saw through the layers of pain and insecurity, recognizing the glimmer of newfound hope and joy that had emerged within me.

Prior to Finn's arrival, our group therapy sessions lacked the opportunity for us to authentically share our stories.

Despite being the very essence of group therapy, we had never truly connected with the reason we were all there. However, Finn refused to settle for surface-level interactions. He pushed us beyond our comfort zones, encouraging us to embrace vulnerability and embrace new experiences.

One day, during a captivating session of art therapy, Finn surprised us by composing a song. With infectious enthusiasm, he gathered us outside, where a variety of musical instruments awaited us. Seated in a circle on the lush grass, Finn assigned each of us a different instrument and provided instructions on how to contribute to the song. As his melody unfolded, our voices and instruments blended harmoniously, filling the air with an ethereal beauty.

You are, you are beautiful.
You are, you are beautiful.
You are, you are lovely.
You are, you are lovely.
We are here with friends today.
We are here with friends today.
Let us hear what you have to say.
Let us hear what you have to say.

In that serene moment, we were not just individuals battling our own internal struggles, but a united group of friends, joined together in solidarity. Finn's creation transcended mere music; it became an anthem of self-worth and collective strength.

As we sang, Finn's unwavering belief in the power of expression and connection became palpable. His song symbolized not only our own individual beauty and worth but also the importance of sharing our voices and stories. It was a testament to the transformative effects of compassion, community, and the tireless efforts of one extraordinary person who had dedicated himself to our healing journey.

Even after meeting Finn, things at the center didn't entirely improve. Eventually, both my mom and I came to the realization that the treatment center was failing to provide the support and guidance I desperately needed. Despite their insistence that I continue with the program, we made the difficult decision to walk away. It became clear that I needed to take control of my own recovery and seek alternative paths to healing.

Healing on my own was not an easy journey. I had a lot of ups and downs. What did I do first? I asked myself; what is really causing my eating disorder? For me, it was my anxiety. Anytime I felt anxious, I lost my appetite. I could have easily said, "I'm going to just get rid of everything that is making me feel anxious." But would that have helped me improve in any way? The short answer is no. When you avoid or put off situations that cause anxiety, you are just prolonging the adrenaline. Instead you need to face your anxiety head on. This is not something that will be easy, nor will it happen overnight. But the more you take steps outside of your comfort zone. Things that once caused panic, now will barely cause an anxious thought. The next thing I asked myself was; what are my triggers? What makes me not want to eat or not feel hungry. I decided to get rid of what made me feel bad about myself. Such as negative people. I cut all of the toxicity out of my life. Ask yourself these questions, and really process them. Even write them down if you need to. Try not to be overwhelmed with the process. There will always be setbacks. But with time, and attentiveness, you will recover.

SIX

Working Through Anxiety

After completing my treatment at the facility, my mother believed it would be beneficial for me to find a job. At the time, I was a fifteen-year-old struggling to reintegrate into the outside world, and my mom thought a job would provide a healthy distraction. The idea seemed plausible, but as I began searching for suitable positions, I encountered numerous obstacles. Most of the jobs I was interested in, such as those at Hollister or American Eagle, required applicants to be at least sixteen or eighteen years old. Unfortunately, I still had six months to go before reaching one of those milestones. Nevertheless, my mom and I were determined to find a solution.

One day, my cousin Estelle invited us to meet her and her kids at the beach. It was a casual get-together, but during our conversation, Estelle mentioned that the restaurant where she worked was currently hiring. She suggested that even though I was younger than the typical age requirement, they might make an exception given their urgent need for "food runners." Intrigued by the possibility, I decided to pursue it. The next step was attending an interview, which was an entirely new experience for me. The nerves were overwhelming, but the questions were relatively simple, and to my surprise, I was offered the job on the spot.

Excited and anxious, I embarked on my first job at Labelle's Winery as a food runner. However, it soon became apparent that this position was not for me. The role demanded exceptional memory skills and the ability to keep up with a fast-paced environment, both of which overwhelmed me. Recognizing my struggles, my supervisors made the decision to switch my role to that of a hostess and table busser. While this change was a slight improvement, I still found myself grappling with intense anxiety while on the job.

My responsibilities as a hostess included answering phone calls and seating customers. Dealing with hungry and sometimes impatient patrons proved to be a daunting task, worsening my anxiety. The pressure and demands of the job infiltrated every aspect of my life, even while I was attending classes at school. It was a constant battle to keep my mind focused on my studies rather than worrying about my performance at work.

One particular day stands out vividly in my memory. I was assigned the task of putting away freshly washed glasses. As expected, the glasses were slippery, and being only four feet and eleven inches tall, reaching the high shelves presented a significant challenge. Unfortunately, this time, my grip faltered, and a glass slipped from my hand, crashing onto the floor in a racket of shattered fragments. While incidents like this were not uncommon, the timing of it was particularly unfortunate. The entire kitchen staff, wedding staff, and my bosses happened to be present, their eyes fixed on me. As someone who despises being the center of attention, my face turned red, and I could feel the sting of tears welling up in my eyes. Estelle, ever perceptive, noticed my distress and immediately took action, pulling me aside and guiding me outside to escape the watchful gazes.

Despite the embarrassment and emotional turmoil, I mustered up the courage to return to work the next day. My mother, recognizing the toll the job was taking on my mental health, arranged a meeting with the human resources department to discuss possible accommodations for my anxiety. However, unbeknownst to us, my boss had already made the decision to let me go. It seemed he had concluded that my anxiety made me unfit for the job. He told me I could always come back when I'm in my 20s. His words stung, but I silently challenged his judgment, thinking to myself, "No, thank you. I aspire to be a nurse; I have no desire to work in a restaurant."

Deciding to get my first job was out of my comfort zone. I was an incredibly anxious person all of the time. What I didn't know then, is that there are actually different stages of the comfort zone. First, of course, is the comfort zone itself. This is where we feel safe and in control. Many people, especially dealing with anxiety, fear leaving their little bubble.

The next step outside is the "fear zone". This is where we may lack self-confidence, we may find excuses to avoid such situations, and we may be easily affected by others opinions. This bubble is going to sound uncomfortable. But spending time in this area will actually help you improve. Sure there will be plenty of times where you will want to regress back to your comfort zone. Such as when I decided not to get another job after being let go from Labelle's.

The next bubble is the "learning zone". This is where we now extend the comfort zone. Things that used to seem scary to us, are no longer scary anymore. We are also able to acquire new skills and deal with challenges and problems we may not have been able to before.

The final bubble is the "growth zone". This is where we finally realize aspirations and find purpose. We are also able to set goals for ourselves now that we know we can do anything we set our minds to.

Learning how to move through the stages of our own comfort zones is not trouble-free. It will require a lot of self patience. Although there will be setbacks, you must never give up on yourself.

SEVEN

Breaking the Mold

The annual town fair was a highly anticipated event that brought the entire community together. The middle school's field transformed into a vibrant carnival, bustling with games, thrilling rides, and the tantalizing aromas of fair food. It was during this time that I found myself amidst a close-knit group of friends consisting of three girls: Brielle, Delia, and Laura. Each of them possessed unique characteristics that shaped our dynamic. Brielle was known for her playful sense of humor, Delia exuded confidence despite occasionally relying on others for decision-making, and Laura naturally assumed the role of the group's leader.

Excitement filled the air as the girls and I planned to spend the day at the fair, followed by a sleepover at my house. Their belongings were already at my place, and my mom had graciously dropped us off at the fairgrounds. My intention was to spend the majority of my time with them, but an unexpected twist entered the equation. The previous night, I had mustered the courage to ask Zach, my lifelong crush, if he wanted to hang out with me at the fair—a proposition to which he agreed. Zach, although shy, had harbored feelings for me for quite some time, yet our interactions had been limited. I wondered if this could be the turning point in our story. However, it is important to note that another boy, Jonah, also harbored a strong interest in me. His infatuation verged on obsession, frequently reaching out to my mom on Facebook to express his undying love or lament his perceived rejections.

As we arrived at the fair, the girls and I stuck together, relishing in the joy of meeting friends we hadn't seen since the school year ended. Engrossed in lively conversations, I failed to notice the gradual disappearance of Brielle, Delia, and Laura from our group. Simultaneously, my focus shifted towards locating Zach, I had gone on a few rides with him as well, until he became absent too. Meanwhile, I remained in the company of my friends, blissfully unaware of the girls' escapade to the high school with a group of older boys. Not only had they vanished without informing me, but they had also done so under my mom's supervision. Feeling abandoned and alone, I phoned my mom, who, in her fury, drove to the fairgrounds. She had planned to meet with Zach's mom—longtime acquaintances who often playfully predicted that Zach and I would marry someday.

Eventually, the girls returned to the fair, only to be met with my mom's stern reprimand. They had violated the trust placed in them while under her watchful eye. My mom highlighted the potential consequences of their actions, emphasizing that if they had been involved in a car accident while heading to the high school, she would have been held accountable. From that point on, my interactions with the girls became increasingly strained. I felt invisible in their presence, as if my voice went unheard. They captured moments together in photographs, intentionally excluding me. Furthermore, Zach seemed to vanish entirely, evading any contact with me and shying away whenever our paths crossed.

Simultaneously, unbeknownst to me, Jonah approached my mom in front of Zach's mom during this tumultuous time. This encounter, lasting an astonishing 40 minutes, left my mom without the opportunity to interject. Jonah divulged his past traumas and ardently expressed his belief that I was essential in his life—a deeply awkward situation that only added to the complexity of my experiences.

As the fair drew to a close and it was time to return home, the girls continued to ignore me, their actions revealing an ongoing pattern. Zach, too, ceased responding to my text messages. The weeks turned into months, and the situation remained unchanged. I grappled with the hurt and confusion caused by their abandonment during a time when I needed support the most.

Entering our sophomore year, I continued to exist on the periphery of the girls' lives. Though I sat with them during lunch and walked alongside them in the halls, I remained a ghostly presence, longing for closure. In the meantime, I sought solace in the company of a new group of friends, but the desire for resolution persisted.

Several months later, fate reunited me with Brielle in a shared class. Recognizing the opportunity for a conversation, I promptly requested to speak with her. A mixture of shock and hives appeared on her neck and chest as my question struck a chord within her.

"It was Laura's idea," she admitted, her voice quivering.

"So, you chose to follow rather than be your own person. That makes you no better," I responded, my words tinged with disappointment. "I've known you the longest among all of them, and yet you betrayed me."

Tears welled up in her eyes, but the damage had already been done. Though we never regained our former closeness, we managed to coexist with a modicum of tolerance when necessary. The scars left by their betrayal remained, but through this experience, I began to understand the importance of surrounding myself with genuine friends who would stand by me, even during challenging times.

EIGHT

Escape to Reality

The COVID-19 pandemic was an unprecedented and challenging time that most people would prefer to erase from their memories. Unfortunately, I found myself in the midst of it halfway through my sophomore year. The sudden closure of schools, initially for a two-week period that extended into months, left us grappling with an uncertain and isolated existence. As summer vacation approached, the world remained closed off, and masks became an inescapable part of our daily lives. Desperate for a reprieve from this new reality, my family and I searched for a way to escape the confines of our COVID-dominated existence.

Enter my Auntie Layla and Uncle Chris, who owned a camper that they would frequently move from one campsite to another. They had secured a lot at a campsite not too far from my home, offering us the perfect opportunity to escape for a while. Uncle Chris, known for his quick wit and love for making people laugh, brought a lightheartedness to every situation. And my Auntie Layla was his perfect counterpart, skillfully reining him in when necessary with her gentle nature.

To make our camping adventure even more exciting, my mom suggested that we rent a cabin. However, it wasn't your typical rustic cabin as one might envision. Instead, it was more like an apartment, providing us with a luxurious glamping experience. My cousins Natalie, Ethan, and Eddie had also rented a cabin right across from mine, and we eagerly anticipated spending a few carefree days together at the campsite. This was our chance to escape the suffocating grip of the COVID world. Since we would be spending most of our time outdoors, masks were not required, and for once, life felt refreshingly normal again.

Natalie and Ethan, had brought their furry companions along for the adventure, Smith and Westen. In an attempt to let the dogs burn off some energy, they tied them outside for a short while. Smith, being a lively puppy, dashed around in circles, and in a comical twist of fate, ended up wrapping his wire leash around my legs. I nearly tumbled to the ground, but Natalie quickly grabbed my arm, and Ethan swiftly intervened to untangle Smith from the amusing predicament. Although the wire leash had caused a painful burn on my ankle at the time, it now serves as a small scar that holds a fond and funny memory.

Natalie had always been like an older sister to me, someone I admired and looked up to for guidance on navigating the complexities of growing up and relationships. Besides my mom, she was often the first to recognize when it was time for me to extricate myself from toxic situations, providing invaluable advice and support. Ethan, who is actually Natalie's fiancé and not my cousin, had become an older brother figure in my life over the years. With a strong protective instinct, he always watched out for me, mirroring Natalie's wisdom in knowing when it was time to let go and move on.

My cousin Eddie, Natalie's younger brother, also played the role of an older brother in my life. He was always willing to lend an ear whenever I needed to vent, offering his unique brand of advice. More often than not, he would find a way to inject humor into my situations, lightening the mood and providing me with a fresh perspective.

Spending time with them during our camping adventure filled me with excitement. We enjoyed bonding over bonfires, cruising around in golf carts, engaging in playful games, and even organizing epic water balloon fights with our younger cousins. Additionally, my cousin Xander joined in on the fun. Over the past few years, we had developed a close bond. With a shared interest in the medical field, Xander always provided the encouragement I needed to pursue my dreams and succeed in my chosen path.

Together, my family brought joy, laughter, and a sense of normalcy to an otherwise challenging time. Our camping escapade provided a much-needed respite from the COVID-19 world, allowing us to reconnect, create cherished memories, and temporarily escape the uncertainties that had come to define our lives.

NINE

Breaking Down Barriers

Although my own cheerleading days had become a distant memory, a new chapter in my cheer journey unfolded when I discovered my younger cousin Ella's involvement in an adaptive cheer team. Ella, a vibrant soul who faced the challenges of being deaf and autistic with unwavering resilience, captivated my heart from the moment I witnessed her radiating joy on the cheer floor. Her intelligence and quick wit shined and it was in those moments that I realized the transformative power of inclusive cheerleading.

Auntie Julia, Ella's mother, not only served as a beacon of love and support but also donned the hat of head coach for the adaptive cheer team. Under her guidance, the team fostered an environment where individuals with various disabilities could experience the exhilaration of cheerleading. A crucial component of this inclusive approach was the integration of "peer partners," individuals like myself who acted as allies and mentors to the athletes, assisting them in cheer routines, jumps, stunts, and tumbling during competitions and games.

In my first year as a peer partner, I had the privilege of being paired with a delightful young girl named Isla, who possessed an infectious smile and a giggle that could light up even the darkest room. Isla faced the daily challenges of Rett syndrome, a neurological disorder that affected her ability to communicate verbally. Yet, in her own unique way, she embraced life with a joy that was truly inspiring.

As I entered the cheer gym alongside Isla, her eyes lit up with an undeniable spark of recognition and anticipation. It was as if she knew that together, we would embark on an extraordinary journey filled with laughter and shared triumphs. The simplicity of her joy, unencumbered by words, reminded me of the profound impact a genuine connection could have, transcending the limitations of language.

Throughout our practices and performances, I witnessed the purest form of happiness radiate from Isla. Her contagious enthusiasm reverberated through every routine, infusing our movements with an energy that transcended the realm of mere cheerleading. As we tumbled and cheered side by side, a silent symphony of shared passion and mutual encouragement enveloped us, creating a bond that required no spoken words.

In the midst of every routine, I would catch glimpses of Isla's bright eyes fixated on me, her gaze radiating a profound sense of gratitude. It was in those moments that I understood the power of presence, of being a constant source of support for someone who relied on the unwavering dedication of those around her. Through the language of love and understanding, we transcended the barriers that separated us, forging a connection that went beyond the realm of cheerleading.

As my second year on the team approached, my role evolved into that of an assistant coach. This new position allowed me to immerse myself even deeper in the world of adaptive cheerleading, enabling me to contribute to the choreography of our routines and assist in teaching the counts to the athletes. The responsibility was not one I took lightly, as

I understood the profound impact each routine would have on the athletes, their families, and the broader community.

Together with Aunt Jessa and the other coaches, we worked hard to create routines that showcased the unique abilities and strengths of each athlete. We marveled at the incredible determination and growth displayed by the team, as they fearlessly defied societal expectations and embraced their own individuality. Each practice was a testament to the transformative power of adaptive cheerleading, as the athletes embodied resilience, perseverance, and a shared sense of purpose.

In the final moments before competitions, as nerves tinged the air with anticipation, I would witness a sea of brightly colored uniforms and smiling faces. Each athlete, regardless of their disability, radiated a quiet confidence that could only be born from the unwavering support and encouragement received from their teammates, coaches, and peer partners. The unity forged through adaptive cheerleading extended far beyond the realm of routines and trophies—it became a sanctuary of belonging, where differences were celebrated and individual strengths were elevated.

The journey of adaptive cheerleading had left an indelible mark on my heart—a mark that would forever remind me of the transformative power of inclusion and the potential for triumph that lies within every individual, regardless of their perceived limitations. It was through the joyous laughter, the shared victories, and the unspoken connections that I realized the profound impact a group of dedicated individuals could have when united in the pursuit of a common goal.

As I reflect upon my time as a peer partner and assistant coach, I am reminded of the extraordinary courage and strength exhibited by Ella, Isla, and the entire team. They taught me that our differences need not divide us, but rather, they should be celebrated as the threads that weave together the vibrant tapestry of humanity. The athletes of the adaptive cheer team will forever hold a special place in my heart, serving as a constant reminder that in the pursuit of inclusivity, every voice deserves to be heard and every spirit deserves to soar.

TEN

Searching for Purpose

Amidst the challenges I faced, one aspect of my life that
brought me immense joy was the art of hair and makeup. It was
a passion I harbored and dreamt of turning into a career as a
cosmetologist. I envisioned myself helping individuals prepare
for memorable events like proms and weddings, using my
creativity to enhance their natural beauty. My collection of
makeup palettes and hair accessories grew, and I eagerly
practiced my skills on mannequin heads whenever I found a
spare moment. However, there came a day when I
contemplated abandoning it all. The decision to let go of my
dreams in cosmetology was partially influenced by the
aftermath of ending my relationship with Jack. I felt the need to
sever any connections to him, as he had always criticized my

aspirations in the field. Strangely enough, I found gratitude for his disparaging remarks because they ignited a fire within me. This fire propelled me towards a different path, one that fueled my desire to help others in a much different way.

Nursing had previously crossed my mind at different stages of my life. I had always been fascinated by the intricacies of the human body and held a deep admiration for science. Yet, it was only after enduring an abusive relationship, grappling with PTSD, and battling an eating disorder that my passion to become a nurse truly ignited. The desire to make a difference in the lives of those who were not only physically unwell but also emotionally wounded became strong.

You should turn your challenges into something you are passionate about. I want to help others. I'm going into a field that revolves around that factor. I am also writing this book. For you and for many others alike. You are not alone.

During my junior year of high school, an opportunity arose to participate in a Health Science Program offered by another school. It presented a chance for me to gain insight into the healthcare industry and confirm whether it was truly the path I wanted to pursue before embarking on my college journey. However, acceptance into the program hinged on my academic performance, so I dedicated myself to achieving excellent grades. The day I received the acceptance letter in the mail remains etched in my memory. Overwhelmed with emotion, I dropped to the floor, tears streaming down my face, and felt an overwhelming sense of pride for the hard work I had invested to attain this opportunity.

The first year of the program proved to be far from easy. We delved into the realm of medical terminology and immersed ourselves in the intricate knowledge of anatomy and physiology, which I found to be utterly fascinating. Unlike my experience with regular high school classes, where good grades came effortlessly, I quickly realized that the material I encountered in this program demanded a significantly greater level of effort and dedication. Throughout this journey, my anxiety levels soared, but I was fortunate to have an exceptional teacher, Mr. Benson, by my side. His guidance and mentorship were invaluable. At various intervals throughout the year, we underwent SPUR assessments, providing us with constructive feedback on our performance in the class and highlighting areas for improvement. During my first SPUR I had expressed how I didn't like to be called on without raising my hand. Mr. Benson's response was,

"I'm still going to call on you. You will not be able to become more confident if you do not feel a little uncomfortable at times."

Under the guidance of my teacher, I experienced a transformative journey in conquering my anxiety. He encouraged me to actively participate in class, not just by asking questions but also by offering answers. This seemingly small step allowed me to regain control over my anxiety and realize that I possessed the ability to overcome it. Moreover, Mr. Benson imparted two invaluable lessons that have resonated with me ever since. He taught me that anxiety arises from caring deeply about something and that anxiety and excitement are essentially the same physiological response, differing only in how they are perceived. These insights transformed my perspective, fueling my determination to confront anxiety head-on and convert it into a catalyst for personal growth.

Driven by my newfound resilience, I sought opportunities to challenge myself further. Joining the club HOSA (Health Occupations Students of America) presented a platform for me to embrace my adventurous spirit. HOSA offered a range of competitive events across various professions, and I opted to participate in the Nursing Assisting event. To my surprise and elation, I secured third place at the state level—a remarkable accomplishment. This achievement filled me with a sense of pride unlike any other, as it not only proved my own self-doubts wrong but also shattered the disparaging beliefs Jack had imposed on me. The arduous efforts I had invested in year one of the program had paid off, I had been invited to return for year two. The prospect of continuing my journey in health science excited me, as it would propel me closer to my ultimate goal of becoming a nurse.

During the second year of the program, we were afforded greater flexibility in choosing our focus of study. We had the option to enroll in an Emergency Medical Technician course, a Licensed Nursing Assistant (LNA) course, or an Extended Learning Opportunity that allowed us to shadow professionals in various healthcare fields. I applied for the LNA course.

Throughout year two, I proactively continued to confront my anxiety, seeking opportunities that required me to step outside my comfort zone. Every time I expressed this desire to my year two teacher, Mrs. Jean, she greeted my aspirations with a mixture of surprise, excitement, and unwavering support. Her belief in my abilities, even when I doubted myself, became a source of inspiration. I embraced the role of ambassador for my program, sharing my experiences and insights with prospective students, extolling the program's remarkable benefits.

The LNA course required completing clinical hours at a nursing home. While most of my classmates could schedule their clinicals during the week, certain constraints prevented me from doing so due to the distance I lived from the facility. Fortunately, another classmate named Molly faced a similar predicament. Through Mrs. Jean's support and ingenuity, we were able to complete our clinical hours at a different nursing home on weekends, forging a unique bond as we navigated the challenges together.

Clinical rotations proved to be a riveting experience. Initially, we felt overwhelmed, as we were thrust into the environment and had to navigate it independently. This trial-by-fire approach seemed daunting at first, but it ultimately proved instrumental in our growth and development. We learned through hands-on experience, finding solutions to problems without constant guidance. My gratitude towards Molly grew as I observed her confidence, outgoing nature, and ability to advocate for herself and others.

As my senior year progressed, I faced the daunting task of applying to colleges. Determined to pursue my passion for nursing, I meticulously prepared applications for six schools. Among these options, Rivier University held a special place in my heart. Renowned for its exceptional nursing school and its supportive faculty, Rivier University offered the ideal environment for me to flourish.

Beyond the significance of grades, the college essay portion of the application process emerged as a pivotal opportunity for me to convey my personal journey and aspirations. I recognized the essay's potential to provide colleges with a deeper understanding of who I am as an individual. With great determination, I set out to articulate my experiences and growth, demonstrating how I had triumphed over adversities and discovered my unwavering passion for nursing.

~~~~

Only 5% of individuals with an eating disorder ever recover. Those were the words I heard one inclement morning, while sitting with a nurse at an eating disorder treatment facility. I had been battling anorexia nervosa for almost 3 years, and I desperately wanted to recover because promptly, my health depended on it. I never thought that this unrealistic desire for perfection would leave me in this destructive cycle but the facts were there. The effects of malnourishment were insidious, and I was paying the price. Throughout my entire recovery, the words of this nurse stuck with me like a leech that I couldn't shake off. To this day I'm still unsure where this nurse got the 5% from since research suggests that anywhere between 60-80% of eating disorder patients going through treatment recover. To be more specific in my case, 46% of anorexia patients fully recover. Before this moment I was very hesitant to recover even though I knew that's what I needed. But something about those words lit a fire of motivation inside me that nothing could ever put out.

Despite medical advice, I left the facility and started the recovery process on my own. For some, this decision may seem foolish, however, it was the right path for me. No matter how badly I wanted to avoid any medical professionals, it seemed like I was always around nurses. All of them were much different from the nurse I had met at the facility. They were all empathetic, encouraging, and even humorous at times. But the one thing they all had in common, was their passion for helping others. As long as I can remember I've always loved helping those around me. I'm known to be someone who is extremely empathetic and supportive. Being surrounded by so many incredible nurses helped me realize that this enormous struggle I was encountering in my daily life actually led me straight to my purpose. This realization inspired me to recover because I now recognized that I wouldn't be able to help others if I didn't help myself first.

To someone else, the negativity that was shown by the nurse at the eating disorder facility would have completely put them down and made them feel hopeless. But I felt empowered and motivated to recover in order to prove her wrong. Now, I have proved her wrong, and found my way.

~~~~

Due to my unwavering determination to attend Rivier University, I decided to participate in their Early Acceptance Program. This unique opportunity allowed me to personally deliver my applications and essays to the university, followed by an interview with an Admissions Counselor. After the interview, I eagerly embarked on a tour of the campus, anxiously awaiting the results that would be delivered to me on the spot. The moment I received my acceptance, elation washed over me, knowing that my dream of attending Rivier had become a reality. However, even with this incredible achievement, I remained curious about the outcomes from the other colleges to which I had applied.

As the results trickled in, I received acceptance letters from Saint Anselm College, Colby Sawyer College, Massachusetts College of Pharmacy and Health Sciences (MCPHS), and Franklin Pierce University. However, there was one unexpected surprise among the list—Dartmouth College, an Ivy League institution. Although Dartmouth did not have a nursing program, I had applied on a whim, driven by curiosity and the desire to see what might unfold.

To my astonishment, I was granted an interview with Dartmouth, an opportunity that both thrilled and intimidated me. During the interview, I found myself grappling with unfamiliar vocabulary and complex concepts that left me feeling unsure of my performance. Refusing to appear ignorant, I did my best to provide thoughtful responses based on my understanding of the questions asked.

While I will never know the outcome of my Dartmouth application, I made the decision to withdraw it before the official decision day arrived. This choice was driven by my commitment to Rivier and the urgency to secure my financial aid and scholarships. Although I may forever wonder what could have transpired, the fact that I was granted an interview alone serves as a point of pride and validation.

Additionally, I competed in the Nursing Assisting event at HOSA once again, triumphing with a first-place finish at the state level. This achievement earned me the opportunity to go to Nashville, Tennessee, to compete at the Internationals.

My trip to Nashville was an extraordinary experience that left an indelible mark on my memories. The opportunity to meet and interact with people from various states was truly fascinating. Each state had its own unique pin, which sparked the tradition of pin trading. I found myself amassing a collection of pins from different states, which I eagerly planned to bring back home with me. While there were only a few students from other countries, I discovered that they were somewhat reluctant to part with their pins, resulting in my inability to acquire any international pins. However, amidst the assortment, there was one pin that captivated my attention—the

Texas pin. With its silver glitter and belt buckle design, it became the coveted pin that everyone desired, but no one wanted to trade. My determination eventually led me to a middle schooler who was willing to part with it, albeit at a price. I happily agreed to pay him $8 for the pin, a sum that seemed inconsequential to me but sparked excitement in him.

The Gaylord Opryland Resort, our accommodation during the trip, was nothing short of grandeur. With its vast expanse, numerous restaurants, and shops, as well as a sprawling convention center, we found ourselves ensconced in a world of possibilities within the confines of the hotel. There was an abundance of activities and entertainment available, rendering it unnecessary for us to venture outside. Although I had to navigate the hotel by myself on a few occasions, which initially seemed daunting, it provided me with a sense of independence that I relished.

The Opening Ceremony of the event was a moment that will forever be etched in my mind. It served as the catalyst for the excitement that lay ahead during the week. The ceremony commenced with the "Parade of Flags," where representatives from each state or country took the stage, waving their respective flags proudly. I had the honor of representing New

Hampshire and underwent flag training to ensure I waved it with precision and grace. During this time, I forged connections with friends from other states, further enriching my experience. Finally, the moment arrived when I walked onto the stage, holding the New Hampshire flag, in front of a colossal audience of 10,000 people—a feat that obliterated my anxiety and left me feeling triumphant.

The main HOSA event required me to complete a 50-question exam that was mostly anatomy. Regrettably, I had not dedicated much time to studying as I viewed the trip itself as a reward for my hard work leading up to internationals. As the day progressed, the eagerly anticipated results of the exam were announced earlier than expected. With bated breath, I opened the email, scanning fervently to find my name among the successful candidates who had qualified for the second round. To my astonishment and delight, my name appeared on the list. Out of the 200 participants who took the same exam, only 20 were chosen to move forward. It was evident that my efforts had paid off, and I felt a surge of accomplishment.

The second round of the competition involved practical skills. Once again, I had not dedicated sufficient time to studying for this segment, leaving me anxious about the tasks I would need to perform in front of the judges. Alongside other participants in my event, I embarked on a bus ride to a nearby college, where we would undergo this phase. The waiting period proved to be nerve-wracking, as we all anxiously sat in a room, with groups of three being summoned every 15 minutes. As the room gradually emptied, my apprehension grew. Before I knew it, it was my turn. Although I felt reasonably comfortable with the skills presented to me, nervousness clouded my mind, causing me to momentarily forget some minor steps. Nevertheless, I remained optimistic and pushed forward.

While I did not receive the opportunity to ascend the grand stage or receive a medal due to not placing in the top 10, I did achieve 11th place worldwide—a remarkable achievement of which I was immensely proud.

Moreover, during the trip, my friends and I explored downtown Nashville, which proved to be a mesmerizing experience. It was there that I developed a newfound appreciation for country music and indulged in delectable southern cuisine. Nashville became the catalyst for my personal growth, instilling in me a sense of confidence and independence that would resonate within me long after the trip concluded.

In retrospect, my journey to Nashville was an amalgamation of thrilling encounters, unexpected triumphs, and self-discovery. The bonds forged, the skills honed, and the experiences gained during this adventure have left an indelible impact on my character and fueled my desire to continue exploring and embracing new opportunities. I turned my struggles into my strength.

Finding our purpose can oftentimes be an overwhelming topic. But it can be determined with these four simple questions, which I will lay out in a very similar way to how I processed them.

"What do you love?"

"I love to help others. I enjoy making others feel better and making them happy."

"What are you good at?"

"I am good at helping others. I have an empathetic nature about me, where I can put myself into others' shoes. This helps me be the best for them.

"Can you be paid?"

"There are plenty of professions that involve helping others. But the one I am the most drawn to is nursing. Due to my love of science as well."

"Lastly, does the world need it?"

"Yes. Specifically, the world needs nurses to care for patients. The healthcare setting would not function without them. The world also needs caring and empathetic individuals to uplift during challenging times."

Once you have answered all of these questions, and hopefully find a connection between them all, you have found your purpose. Use it wisely. The world needs you.

ELEVEN

Sour

Junior year, when I embarked on the health science program, a world of new possibilities opened up before me. Interacting with students from other schools provided a refreshing opportunity to redefine myself. At this new school, nobody knew about the hardships I had faced at my home-school, granting me a chance to forge new connections and let go of the past.

It was during those initial weeks that I encountered Andrew, a classmate who showed a keen interest in getting to know me better. Despite his apparent attraction, I approached the situation with caution, as I had developed a lingering sense of unease whenever a guy showed interest in me. It wasn't exactly anxiety, but rather an instinctual gut feeling that urged caution. However, he was persistent

Curiosity eventually got the better of me, and I decided to engage in conversation with Andrew. In those early conversations, we both shared glimpses of our past traumas, finding solace in our ability to confide in one another. Although I held back certain details, as I wasn't ready to fully disclose the extent of my past, Andrew took it upon himself to proclaim that he would help me recognize my self-worth and ensure I would never endure mistreatment again. Little did I know at the time that his promises would prove empty.

As time went on, my desire to avoid a romantic entanglement with Andrew persisted. Despite my reservations, we continued to engage in daily text conversations. However, things took a gradual turn for the worse. He began pressuring me to divulge every intricate detail of my past, demanding a level of disclosure I was not comfortable with providing. Firmly standing my ground, I refused to yield to his relentless prodding.

"If you can't respect that I'm not ready to talk about something then that's not okay." I would say.

As the months went by, the toxic dynamics of my relationship with Andrew only intensified, and it became increasingly clear that his behavior was far from healthy. Whenever I resisted his demands or questioned his actions, he would respond with silence, intentionally ignoring me for hours on end. This emotional manipulation left me feeling anxious and uncertain, as I desperately sought his approval and feared the consequences of his anger.

Adding to the distress, Andrew would frequently resort to making alarming threats of self-harm, using this as a means to exert control over me. These episodes would be followed by prolonged periods of silence, leaving me in a state of emotional turmoil. It was a distressing cycle that had a significant impact on me, coincidentally occurring during meal times and causing a loss of appetite due to the heightened stress.

Month after month, I found myself trapped in this tumultuous relationship. The weight of responsibility to prevent Andrew from harming himself became an immense burden. The pattern of emotional manipulation, combined with his threats, intensified my anxiety and forced me to prioritize his well-being over my own. It was an exhausting cycle that further eroded my sense of self-worth and perpetuated a toxic dynamic.

Against my better judgment, and foolishly believing that making our relationship official would somehow alleviate the problems, I decided to give in at the end of my junior year. However, the change I had hoped for never materialized. If anything, the situation only worsened as Andrew continued to exert control over me. He coerced me into opening up about my past, a step I had not been ready to take, and his response to my vulnerability was far from supportive or understanding. Instead, he dismissed my experiences, claiming that I had scared him away. It was yet another tactic employed to maintain power.

When Andrew visited my house for our weekly family dinner, bonfire, and game night, the atmosphere became tense. Natalie, Ethan, and Eddie, keen observers of the changes in my demeanor, noticed how Andrew would suddenly grow silent, causing me to question myself and withdraw. This troubled my cousins greatly, to the point where they were reluctant to join these gatherings if they knew he would be present.

Andrew had a fondness for hiking, a pastime that my mother viewed with suspicion and concern. She had noticed unsettling signs in his behavior, which led her to worry about my safety. Her fear took a dark turn, as she became convinced that he might push me off a cliff during one of our hikes. Although I dismissed her concerns at first, I couldn't ignore the not-so-subtle signs of potential danger emanating from Andrew. Everytime I would be with him in the car, he would say,

"You know, I could just kidnap you right now. No one would ever know where you are."

The extent of Andrew's disturbing behavior and the escalating threats he made were deeply unsettling. Despite his attempts to pass them off as jokes, he managed to convince me of the genuine danger he posed. He would describe in chilling detail how he would kill me and dispose of my body, leaving me filled with a sense of terror and uncertainty. Any indication that I doubted his intentions would unleash a storm of rage.

It wasn't just his words that triggered concern; his treatment of my dog, Charlie, raised red flags for both my mother and I. Rather than petting him affectionately, Andrew would handle Charlie in a peculiar manner. He would lay him on his back, stretching out his limbs and sometimes placing his hand on his neck. In fleeting moments when our attention was diverted, we couldn't help but worry that he might harm or even kill my dog. The mere thought sent shivers down our spines, and deep down, we knew that Andrew possessed the capacity to carry out such heinous acts.

Adding to the chilling atmosphere, there were instances when we were alone together and he would tightly grip my arm, his voice dripping with malice as he reminded me,

"You know it would actually be really easy for me to break your bones."

The veiled threats and the physical intimidation were undeniably disturbing, creating an environment of fear and unease that permeated our interactions. The revelation that Andrew had been diagnosed as a psychopath by a medical professional only intensified our concerns.

As senior year unfolded, the same patterns persisted. However, a new dilemma emerged between Andrew and I. Still haunted by the trauma inflicted by Jack, I had maintained a reluctance to engage in anything related to sex. I refused to surrender control or compromise my boundaries, as Andrew had not earned the right to experience that intimate part of me. But as he forged friendships with other guys who openly discussed their relationships, jealousy consumed him, and he directed his frustrations toward me.

Andrew's jealousy manifested as manipulation, gradually wearing down my defenses. Eventually, I succumbed to the same actions I had allowed Jack to take, not because I wanted to but because tolerating it seemed to be the only role left for me in our deteriorating relationship.

On his birthday, Andrew tried to convince me to break down my boundaries. I mustered the courage to explain to him how this expectation triggered my PTSD. In response, he callously accused me of ruining his birthday and making things awkward. Rather than allowing his words to affect me, I felt a surge of pride for standing up for myself and asserting my boundaries, refusing to compromise my well-being for the sake of his desires. It was a small victory, but an important one, as it affirmed my worth and my commitment to prioritizing my own needs and healing.

My battle with insecurities persisted, and Andrew's response to my body image concerns only fueled my self-doubt. Whenever I mentioned something I disliked about my appearance, his insensitive and dismissive advice was to simply work out.

"Just do squats if you want a bigger butt, or do sit-ups for a flatter stomach."

His remarks were not only insensitive but also deeply hurtful. I was unaware at the time that working out alone wouldn't address the root of my insecurities. It was a complex combination of factors that would only become apparent to me later on.

What troubled me even more was Andrew's close friendships with other girls. They would spend time together one-on-one frequently, engaging in activities such as hiking with Hailey, going out to dinners with Kimberly, or going on bike rides with Meredith. These friendships had developed after we started dating, which made me uneasy. If they had been childhood friends, I might have viewed the situations differently. However, these hangouts gradually transformed into sleepovers, adding to my growing sense of discomfort and mistrust.

Andrew possessed a deeply ingrained competitive nature. He always strived to be the best, the smartest, and the one who could amass the most wealth. While such ambition might be admirable in someone driven by personal success, for Andrew, it seemed to revolve around outshining others and making them feel inferior. Even my grades, consistently in the 90s, were "not good enough" according to his standards. Unless they were a perfect 100%, they held no value in his eyes. While his relentless push for me to excel academically had its merits, it left me feeling perpetually unsatisfied. Despite achieving good grades, I couldn't find a sense of pride or fulfillment in my accomplishments.

I vividly remember a time when Andrew became upset with me for expressing my aspirations of becoming a Nurse Practitioner in the future. His envy was palpable. He too had aspirations of becoming a Nurse Practitioner, but he desired to earn the most money if we were to ever get married. Once again, his primary focus was on establishing his superiority over others, emphasizing financial success over personal fulfillment.

As prom approached, I found myself seriously contemplating ending my relationship with Andrew. The toll of being mistreated had become exhausting, and even my mom, who witnessed my struggles, urged me to break free from this toxic dynamic. She believed that my person awaited me at Rivier University. However, I doubted the possibility of finding someone different since my past experiences had conditioned me to expect the same treatment. Thus, I chose to stick it out, clinging to the hope that things might improve.

~~~~

3/22/22

For when I decide I need this…

I can't do this anymore. I love you to death and I want you to know that, but I just can't handle this anymore. You put me through an enormous amount of stress and I'm at my breaking point. I can't continue to grow and move forward if I'm constantly feeling like I have to adjust myself for you. I always feel like everything I do is wrong. You always get mad at me or frustrated when things don't go your way. This relationship is not one sided nor should it be, there's two of us so if there is a disagreement there should be compromise. I'm done crying myself to sleep. I'm done crying at school. I'm done crying when my family is over. I'm done crying. This hurts me more than you know. But it won't hurt worse than what you already put me through. I wish you treated me the same way you did at the beginning. Never once did you take your emotions out on me, but that quickly changed. And I had already fallen for you. If I was smarter I would have never put myself through this again. I'm emotionally drained. I really wanted you to be my forever. But I can't be with someone who is going to get mad at me and shut down after every minor inconvenience. I always wanted to treat you the same way you treated me. But I always thought about how you would feel after the fact. My heart was too big to put you through that. To give you a taste now, you'd get frustrated with me and go to sleep. You'd probably sleep amazing too, knowing that you have complete control over the girl you supposedly "love." Meanwhile, my heart races, I panic, I cry, I want to scream. I genuinely think about hurting myself because you constantly make me feel like I'm the worst person in the universe. I can't ever do anything right. I always do something wrong. And God, I just can't take it anymore.

I've given you chance after chance, and you've done nothing to make things better. I love you so much and this is literally killing me. But we need to be away from each other. We shouldn't be together anymore. I don't think I'm the one for you. I don't do anything right and there must be someone out there who can. We are on different walks of life.

~~~~

Prom night turned into a nightmarish ordeal. The evening began with Andrew's reluctance to take pictures. He had never been fond of being photographed, so the few pictures we managed to capture together appeared awkward and lacked the genuine connection I longed for. Fortunately, I had also taken individual pictures, allowing me to commemorate the occasion in a more positive light. I wore a beautiful light pink dress adorned with delicate tulle, sparkling embellishments, and enchanting floral details that gracefully trailed along the floor. After the initial picture fiasco, we embarked on our journey to prom.

Initially, the night didn't seem too bad. I met with a group of close friends, and we took pictures together, sharing laughter and excitement. However, as the music grew louder and the energy intensified, the true issues began to surface. Andrew adamantly insisted on staying outside, refusing to enter the venue to dance or even stand by my side. Left with no choice, I ventured inside and joined my friends on the dance floor, desperately trying to immerse myself in the joyous atmosphere. However, my heart grew heavy with envy as I witnessed other couples reveling in each other's company, making the most of the evening. Overwhelmed with sadness, I made my way outside, determined to persuade Andrew to join me inside. Little did I know that our encounter would lead to him abruptly ending our relationship, right in the midst of prom.

Devastated, tears streamed down my face, and my friends, who were rightfully outraged by Andrew's actions, had enough of his games. Brooklyn, never one to hold back, unleashed her fury upon him, passionately expressing her disdain for his behavior and making it clear that he didn't belong in this space. He walked away, preparing to leave. Driven by a mix of confusion, heartache, and a desperate need for closure, I ran after him, navigating the stairs while carefully holding the train of my dress and trying not to stumble in my heels. It may seem irrational to chase after someone who broke my heart during prom, but in that moment, I yearned for an explanation, a glimmer of hope that would somehow mend the shattered pieces of my emotions. We found a secluded spot within the venue to have a conversation, as he had no immediate means of departure since his car was parked at my house, and my mom had dropped us off earlier in the evening. Despite the semblance of reconciliation, a few days later, our relationship officially came to an end.

The story doesn't conclude there; unfortunately, there's more to unravel. Following our abrupt breakup, Andrew and I spent an entire month apart, devoid of any contact. During that time, significant events unfolded in my life. I graduated from high school, marking the end of a chapter and the beginning of a new journey. Additionally, I embarked on a trip to Nashville for HOSA Internationals, a bittersweet experience that allowed me to focus on personal growth. Amidst this emotional turmoil, I found solace in the company of Luke, a friend of Andrew's who had recently undergone a breakup himself. Our shared circumstances created a space for open conversation and mutual support.

Although Luke and I only hung out a few times, I found myself drawn to his seemingly different demeanor. On our first outing, we embarked on a brief hike before indulging in ice cream. It was during these moments that Luke displayed a level of attentiveness and empathetic understanding that I had sorely missed. I confided in him, divulging the painful experiences I had endured with both Jack and Andrew. He responded with a statement that resonated with my hopeful heart.

"I never initiate anything with girls, since you never know what they have gone through."

Naive and longing for understanding, I wholeheartedly believed his words. Our second encounter was equally innocent, consisting of another hike, a shared lunch, and time spent at his lake house. Yet, as the day unfolded, I couldn't ignore the subtle shift in his demeanor. Luke seemed to be waiting for an opportunity to kiss me, and despite my lingering feelings for him, I hesitated. After deciding to take me for a ride on his jetski, he seized the moment, kissing me in the middle of the lake. We retreated to his boat, and continued to kiss. But my discomfort grew as it became apparent that Luke desired a more physical connection. I found myself tensing up, a reaction he noticed and promptly labeled as making things "awkward." The familiarity of this accusation sent a shiver down my spine, evoking memories of similar situations in the past. Following that encounter, Luke and I ceased to spend time together. He had proposed a summer fling, a carefree and commitment-free arrangement, as he was preparing to move out of state for college in the coming months. Declining his proposition, our communication dwindled to a mere trickle.

Not long after, Andrew resurfaced in my life. Although we never officially reconciled or labeled ourselves as a couple again, we began talking and soon found ourselves entangled in a relationship dynamic reminiscent of our previous one. Regrettably, this summer fling with Andrew mirrored our prior experiences, marked by mistreatment and secrecy. Sneaking behind my mother's back became a regrettable necessity as we met up, further deepening the tangled web of emotions and deception.

Yes. I had gone back to an abusive relationship. Even now I am embarrassed to admit it. But it is so normal to do. The reason I had gone back was because I "loved" him. I understand now that I didn't truly love him. And our relationship was far from loving. I stayed and went back because of my idea and hopes of what our relationship could be. But, it is important to understand that abusive relationships never change. It is a constant cycle. The only way to break the cycle is to leave. That is the only way change will occur.

TWELVE

Maternal Manipulation

Most of the damage inflicted upon me during my relationship with Andrew didn't originate from him alone but rather from his mother, Evelyn. Evelyn was a strong-willed woman who had embarked on a solo journey from Greece to the United States at the age of 19. However, her aspirations for both Andrew and I were unreasonably high, steeped in unrealistic expectations.

Andrew's unwavering belief in having no grades lower than 100% can be traced back to Evelyn's influence. I vividly remember walking into their house only to witness Evelyn's berating Andrew over a seemingly trivial high school essay. In the grand scheme of things, such academic endeavors held little significance. Nevertheless, she yearned for her son to embody perfection. Sadly, the pursuit of perfection often exacts a hefty toll, leaving individuals perpetually feeling inadequate. After all, true perfection remains elusive, as our personal definitions of it vary, making it an unattainable goal.

Evelyn consistently belittled my aspirations of becoming a nurse, dismissing it as "just a job." Yet, for me, nursing held a much deeper meaning. It represented my passion and purpose, a calling to aid and support others in their time of need. I yearned to make a difference and provide care to those who required it most. Evelyn, however, insisted that jobs were solely for financial gain.

"You never work a day in your life if you truly enjoy what you are doing," I would counter.

Money held little significance to me. It was the fulfillment I derived from helping others that mattered most. Despite my explanations, Evelyn remained unsupportive, dismissing my chosen path as menial. She would scoff at my ambitions of working as a Licensed Nursing Assistant (LNA) in a nursing home, reducing my role to merely "wiping butts." While it was true that such tasks formed a part of my responsibilities, there was so much more to my role. Beyond the physical care, my interactions with residents involved providing emotional support and fostering a sense of purpose. Many of the individuals I cared for battled profound feelings of hopelessness, contemplating suicide or pleading with God to end their suffering. Witnessing their anguish broke my heart, but I found solace in offering reassurance and reminding them of their value.

"God needs you to be here right now. I need you to be here right now. It's not your time yet," I would tell them.

Striving to uplift their spirits and instill a renewed sense of purpose. Though such encouragement offered temporary respite, it was an ongoing process that required constant reminders and unwavering support. Evelyn's disdain for nursing likely stems from her own deep-seated envy. It's evident that she lacks empathy and the capacity to provide the kind of encouragement and support that nursing requires.

When confronted with my eating disorder, she displayed a profound lack of understanding. An empathetic person would have made an effort to comprehend the struggles I faced, but Evelyn fell short in this regard. Meals at their house became an uncomfortable ordeal. Evelyn would make comments about the quantity of food I consumed or remark on how I appeared to have gained weight. Such behavior only served to heighten the situation, fueling my insecurities and reinforcing negative self-perceptions.

Evelyn's actions were deceptive and underhanded. She would engage in conversations about me behind my back with Andrew, and I would inevitably discover her disparaging remarks. She labeled me as a "bitch" and harbored an irrational hatred towards me, seemingly without any valid reason. This fueled my desire to prove myself to her, to demonstrate my achievements and successes. I would boast about my grades, and college preparations, relishing in the satisfaction of witnessing her frustration. It felt empowering, as if I had gained some semblance of control and silenced her temporarily, if only for a brief moment.

When I received acceptance into Rivier, Evelyn immediately pressured Andrew to apply to the same college. She attempted to convince me countless times to choose an alternative institution so that Andrew could go there instead.

However, I saw through her tactics. Rivier was my dream school, and I was determined not to let go of that opportunity. I vividly recall the day I informed her of my commitment to Rivier, and her anger was visible. From that point on, I made it a point to wear my Rivier hoodies whenever I visited her house, pleasuring the satisfaction of rubbing my accomplishment in her face.

Both Evelyn and my mother shared the opinion that Andrew and I should not attend the same college, a rare point of agreement between them. Looking back, I am grateful that Andrew didn't choose Rivier. It allowed me the space and freedom to establish my own path without the added complications.

Perhaps one of the most bewildering instances that exposed Evelyn's irrationality involved her belief that I was actively trying to get pregnant. This notion was absurd on multiple levels. Firstly, Andrew and I had never had sex. One of the reasons for this was Andrew's fear of an unintended pregnancy. I had shared with him my personal stance that I would not opt for an abortion if I were to become pregnant. It was a statement driven by my own values and beliefs. Unfortunately, Andrew chose to relay this information to his mother, who somehow concluded that I was intentionally seeking pregnancy. It was a baffling and illogical assumption that defied any appearance of reason.

If this chapter shows you anything. It should be how to deal with a bully. That's all Evelyn was. She was jealous of me and attempted to bring me down to build herself up. Whenever you are dealing with a bully of any sort, there are two things you can do. One being, agree with everything they say. Some may disagree with this statement, because you are belittling yourself in the process. But, you don't have to agree with what you are responding with. An example could be; "Annabelle you get the worst grades, and you're honestly not smart." Your response could be, "You are totally right." Say it with confidence. Just enough to get them to shut up.

Or you could take the route I went with; do everything in your power to prove them wrong. This method I feel is more empowering. You not only prove the bully wrong but you also prove your internal doubts wrong in the past. Whatever you do, just never strive for perfection. It is unattainable and will leave you feeling awful. Just always strive to be better than you were the day before.

THIRTEEN

My Mother's Guilt

The pain my mom endured while witnessing me go through abuse was profound and deeply affecting. As a loving mother, it pained her to the core to see her child suffer in such a way. The scars of her own encounters with abuse throughout her life made her aware of the devastating impact it can have on an individual's well-being. Determined to shield me from the same horrors she had endured, she embarked on a journey to break the cycle and ensure that I wouldn't have to experience it as well.

Growing up, I saw firsthand the lengths my mom went to protect me. She became a pillar of strength, employing every resource at her disposal to create a safe and nurturing environment. She made a conscious effort to educate herself about healthy relationships and effective parenting strategies, determined to provide me with the care and love she had yearned for during her own tumultuous upbringing.

Despite her best efforts, there were moments when my mom found herself overwhelmed by the magnitude of the situation. In times of extreme stress or frustration, she may have made decisions or uttered words that were hurtful. I remember a couple of instances when she threatened to leave me at a gas station when I was younger. I believe she thinks more about these memories than I do. They didn't affect me in the way she believes they do.

Moreover, my mom's self-blame for my anxiety demonstrates the depth of her love and compassion. She takes the responsibility of being a parent seriously and wishes nothing but the best for me. However, attributing my anxiety solely to her actions or perceived shortcomings is an oversimplification of a complex issue. Anxiety is a multifaceted condition influenced by various factors, including genetics, environment, and personal experiences. I don't believe anything my mom did caused my anxiety. It's purely just genetic.

Throughout my journey of healing, I have come to realize that my mom played no part in causing the abuse I endured. And I hope that she can realize that one day too. It is a sobering revelation that frees both of us from the burden of guilt and self-blame. We are not responsible for the actions of others, nor can we control the choices they make. Abuse is a choice made by the abuser, and it is essential to separate the responsibility from those who have been victimized.

The key to rebuilding our lives lies in acknowledging the impact of abuse while also recognizing our own resilience and strength. It is crucial for my mom to understand that she is not defined by her past experiences or the mistakes she made along the way. Her commitment to breaking the cycle of abuse and her unwavering love for me are what define our relationship. She provided me with a foundation of love, support, and encouragement.

It is also important for you as the reader to know and truly understand that you are not defined by your past either.

Don't let your hardships control you or be a reminder of the bad. Instead let it build you up and remind you that you are who you are supposed to be.

FOURTEEN

Shame

Jack's pattern of abuse became evident as I was the first victim in his destructive cycle. Gradually, I noticed a recurring pattern among the girls he dated—they would fall into the same trap. Throughout their relationships and even after their inevitable breakups, these girls turned to me for advice and support. Despite my repeated warnings that Jack wouldn't change, they chose to stay with him. I, too, fell into this pattern of denial, discovering firsthand how abuse has a way of pulling you back in, even against your own better judgment.

I once heard an analogy that resonated deeply with me. It compared abuse to a puppy being mistreated by its owner.

After enduring the abuse, the puppy would be showered with treats, toys, and affection. This conditioning led the puppy to tolerate the abuse, knowing that if it endured the cycle, everything would return to a semblance of normalcy, even if only for a fleeting moment. If given the choice between the original abusive owner and a potential new, loving owner, the puppy would inexplicably choose the former. Why? Because the familiar, despite its toxicity, feels safe, while anything new becomes a source of fear and uncertainty. This analogy shed light on the difficulty of leaving abusive relationships, especially for individuals like myself who have a tendency to try to fix things and see the best in others.

The girls who reached out to me shared their own harrowing tales of abuse. None of their stories surprised me, for I knew Jack's true nature. Among them, Millie stood out as a reflection of my past self. She and Jack would break up repeatedly, only to reconcile time and time again. She found it nearly impossible to walk away; she had become emotionally attached to him.

Millie confided in me that Jack had attempted to take her life. They were spending time together in her room when she said something that displeased him. He forcefully pushed her to the ground and wrapped his hands around her neck, choking her. She struggled to breathe, fearing for her life. Hearing her mother approaching, Jack abruptly released his grip and rushed downstairs to get Millie a glass of water. Left sobbing in her room, Millie was forbidden from allowing him back into her room. Jack had also managed to cause her an eating disorder, a revelation that didn't surprise me in the least. His ability to manipulate and control was second nature.

Another girl, Violet, who was two years younger than us, had her first experience with romantic relationships through Jack. Like the rest of us, she possessed a kind, shy, and naive disposition. They dated for a while, and it was only after their breakup that she confided in me. Violet, too, had fallen victim to an eating disorder. While she never explicitly mentioned physical abuse, she did disclose incidents of sexual assault perpetrated by Jack.

I carry a tremendous burden of guilt for what these girls endured. Many others dated Jack, but not all of them shared their stories with me. I often wish I had reported him when I had the chance. He will never change, and it is evident that his behavior has only escalated. I worry for the well-being of his future partners. However, deep down, I hold onto hope that eventually, he will encounter a resilient and courageous girl who can put an end to his destructive cycle.

We are all going to have regrets in life. I've pondered over the idea of going back and changing the past if I could. But now, I would never change the past. Even if I had reported him when I had the chance, there is no way to know for sure whether he would have been punished or justice would have been served. Take this as a lesson, don't dwell on what could have or may have been. You never know if it would have played out how you imagined or not. You can't blame yourself for not knowing, and you also can't live in the past. The best thing to do is move forward.

FIFTEEN

Breaking the Cycle

At the beginning of college, as I embarked on this new chapter of my life, I was still in communication with Andrew. We continued to engage with each other for about a month, but deep down, I had reached a point where I yearned for something different. The exhaustion from being treated as if I were worthless had taken its toll on me, and I was ready to break free from this cycle.

The day we officially ended things felt peculiar. Surprisingly, I didn't feel overwhelmingly upset. There were no floods of tears or emotional breakdowns. It seemed as though I had exhausted all my tears by that point. Throughout the day, he had been attempting to initiate the breakup, and I was tired of begging for appreciation from someone who was incapable of providing it. By the end of the night, he finally sent the text message that marked the official end. He expressed how happy he was that I could "no longer get under his skin." It was yet another instance where he skillfully painted me as the villain in the story. And to make matters worse, he went as far as telling me that I was "fucked up in the head." Despite his desire to remain friends and maintain contact, I knew deep down that it was time to sever ties completely. I understood that staying in contact with him would only allow him to continue exerting control over me. Thus, we parted ways, and I made a firm decision to never speak with him again.

So how exactly do you leave an abusive relationship? First step is realizing what you are going through. This can often come as denial before it's truly accepted. While we are in it, we don't want to believe the person we love could be so cruel. The next step is knowing your worth, and realizing you've had enough. I had dealt with abusive partners for six years of my life before I was done. I realize that so many others put up with abuse for much longer. I was so exhausted, and although change seemed scary and I didn't believe there was different out there, I left. Because I knew I deserved to be treated better. It is also important to remove all contact. If you stay in communication they will use their guilt-tripping and manipulation tactics to pull you back in. This has worked for them time and time again. And the longer you converse with them, the more you are pulled back and eventually entangled back in the cycle.

~~~~

Being a commuter student made it challenging for me to forge new friendships in college. Thankfully, one of my closest friends from high school, Hallie, was also attending Rivier, but she lived on campus. Whenever I had the chance, I made an effort to have lunch with her and her roommate, Lena, at least twice a week. They became a source of comfort and support during this time. Although I had friends on platforms like Snapchat and other social media, I rarely encountered them in person at school since we didn't have any classes together. I confided in my friend Logan, who was also in the nursing program, along with his then-girlfriend Sienna, with whom I was also close. I opened up to him about the deep sense of depression and loneliness that had engulfed me. I explained my struggles with making friends and the recent loss of the only person I had relied on for emotional support. In response, Logan suggested that we plan a study session to go over anatomy and physiology together.

The day of the study session had arrived, and I couldn't help but feel a mix of excitement and anxiety. It was an opportunity not only to have a study buddy for my challenging courses but also to potentially make new friends who were also in the nursing program. However, as the day progressed and the scheduled time drew near, a familiar pit began to form in my stomach. It was the same sensation I had experienced before, right before meeting a new guy for a hangout or a date. But this time, something felt different. I reminded myself that this wasn't a social gathering or a romantic encounter. We were simply getting together to study, so why was this uneasy gut feeling resurfacing?

As I sat in my car, contemplating whether to stay and study or head back home, a text from Hallie illuminated my phone screen.

"Hey are you still here?"

Ultimately, I made the spontaneous decision to join Hallie in her dorm room, disregarding my initial plans with Logan.

Hallie graciously accompanied me to the dining hall, where we met up with Liv once again. We had also met up with two new friends; Bridget and Armando. As we sat down to have dinner, the conversation naturally gravitated toward our shared experiences from high school, particularly involving Jack, whom we had both dated in the past. In a lighthearted manner, I displayed pictures of my ex-boyfriends to my new friends.

"Wow girl, you were doing charity work." laughed Armando.

However, the mood shifted when I expressed my desire to find a boy who would treat me with the respect and kindness I deserved. Bridget scoffed and dismissed the idea, asserting that the boys at Riv were primarily interested in casual hookups and lacked a genuine desire for a serious relationship. Her words struck a chord within me, causing my spirit to dampen. Doubt began to creep in, questioning whether I would ever find the person I longed for within the confines of Riv.

Silently contemplating Bridget's remark, I felt disheartened. The spark of hope I had nurtured was momentarily extinguished, leaving a lingering sense of disappointment. Yet, amidst this internal struggle, Hallie proposed that we attend the ongoing volleyball game. Determined to seize any chance to alleviate my despondency, I swiftly agreed, adjusting my attire. I exchanged my dress for a comfortable pair of shorts and donned a large hoodie, preparing for an evening of socializing and, perhaps, a renewed sense of optimism.

Throughout the volleyball game, my mind was consumed by the lingering doubts triggered by Bridget's earlier comment. Lost in my own thoughts, I found it difficult to engage in conversation or fully immerse myself in the lively atmosphere. All I yearned for was the prospect of genuine happiness and a healthy, fulfilling relationship. After the game concluded, Hallie, Lena, and I decided to venture over to Haywards, a nearby spot renowned for its delicious ice cream.

As we approached the counter to order, I made a sincere offer to pay for Liv's ice cream. However, to my surprise, the employee never requested my card, resulting in a free scoop of ice cream. Though seemingly insignificant, this unexpected gesture managed to lift my spirits ever so slightly.

Taking our indulgences back to the common area of the dorm, we settled down and continued our conversations. Suddenly, a knock on one of the windows disrupted our tranquil setting.

"Let us in, we are locked out!"

Startled, we hurried to open the door, greeted by two boys seeking entry. One of them was Daniel, a familiar face from a few classes we shared, while the other boy was a stranger to me. Although I acknowledged his attractiveness, I didn't dwell on it and simply went on with my night.

It being a Thursday night, Hallie, ever eager to showcase the allure of "Thirsty Thursday," insisted that I experience a taste of the college party scene before departing. Admittedly, I felt a twinge of nervousness, as this would be my first college party and my first party ever. Arriving at the designated dorm room, I noticed only a small gathering of people since it was still early. Many of them were unfamiliar faces, with only a handful being vaguely recognizable from my encounters around campus.

As the party progressed, I couldn't help but notice the boy who Hallie and I had rescued earlier, the cute one, who I had learned was named Blake. To my surprise, he immediately gravitated towards me, engaging me in conversation and eager to stay by my side. This attention struck me as peculiar. With so many friends in the room, why was he choosing to spend his time with me? I couldn't forget how captivated he seemed by my name, repeatedly uttering it aloud and expressing admiration for its beauty.

I immediately turned to Hallie and asked, "Does he have a girlfriend?"

"No, but he just got out of a relationship, she was crazy." she replied.

I then handed my phone to Hallie, so she could add him on my snapchat.

As I turned back to face Blake, he had asked, "Can I get your snapchat?"

"I actually just asked Hallie for it," I said laughing.

"Wow, you weren't even going to let me ask you first." he said while smiling.

Blake's interest in spending time with me persisted, and eventually, we found ourselves in his dorm room. Bridget was also present initially, participating in our conversation. However, she eventually departed, perhaps growing exasperated with Blake's constant compliments about my name. Left alone, Blake unexpectedly opened up, sharing glimpses of his childhood and the battles he had faced. He appeared taken aback and slightly embarrassed by his own vulnerability, having revealed things he had seldom shared with anyone before.

Without hesitation, I reciprocated by revealing my own experiences with abusive relationships, PTSD, and an eating disorder. Blake's expression turned serious, displaying a level of concern and understanding that I had rarely encountered from other boys. It was then that he asked a question that no one else had ever cared to inquire about: "What are your triggers?"

Although I hesitated to provide a direct answer, fearing it could potentially create an awkward moment, I brushed off the question, promising to delve into the topic at a later time. We settled on his bed, as I had been seated on the floor, and I deliberately avoided making eye contact, intuitively sensing that he would lean in for a kiss. When Blake asked why I wasn't looking at him, I was at a loss for words. But after a few minutes of conversation, he mustered the courage to ask if he could kiss me. I obviously said yes, and we continued talking throughout the night. Eventually, he asked if I wanted to stay.

Pausing for a moment, I contemplated the decision. Before seeking permission from my mother, I needed to connect with my own feelings. I awaited that familiar gut feeling, the warning sign that had accompanied my interactions with previous boys. To my astonishment, it never surfaced. For the first time in what felt like an eternity, I felt safe and comfortable hanging out with a boy. I approached my mom and requested to stay in Hallie's room, using the excuse of having an incredibly enjoyable time. She granted permission, expressing her concern about me not having clothes for the next day. Which was ultimately resolved.

That particular night provided significant insight into Blake's character. We had kissed quite a bit, and whenever his hand grazed my waist, I involuntarily tensed up. Immediately, he would stop kissing me and express genuine concern.

"Please let me know if I'm crossing a line, Annabelle. I never want to make you feel uncomfortable," he assured me sincerely.

It was such a stark contrast to my past experiences. Blake's respect for my boundaries and his attentiveness left me amazed. It helped me realize that there are people out there who will respect my boundaries and see my worth.

The following day, Blake continued to engage with me, dispelling my unfounded fear that he would suddenly stop all communication. I had convinced myself of this possibility, influenced by Bri's cautionary remarks from the previous night. However, Blake proved me wrong by consistently conversing with me and expressing a desire to know me better. Our interactions became a daily occurrence. Even though he had recently ended a less-than-ideal relationship and was not looking to rush into another commitment, we both agreed to be loyal to each other in the meantime.

Blake was unlike anyone I had ever known before. His presence in my life brought with it a newfound sense of care and attentiveness that felt both comforting and unfamiliar. When we engaged in conversations, his undivided attention and intentional listening made me feel seen and heard in a way I had never experienced before. It was a refreshing change from the past, where my pleas for reassurance often fell on deaf ears.

In Blake's eyes, I was beautiful, inside and out, and he made sure I knew it. He showered me with compliments, speaking words of affirmation that lifted my spirits and bolstered my self-esteem. Whenever I found it difficult to fully accept his compliments, he devised a simple yet powerful exercise to help me internalize my own beauty.

"Say you are pretty three times," he would gently prompt me.

"I am pretty, I am pretty, I am pretty," I would reply, trying to muster confidence in my words.

If my response lacked conviction or if I rolled my eyes in disbelief, Blake would insist that I start over. He understood the importance of affirming oneself and recognizing one's own worth. He believed that true beauty came from within, and he was determined to help me see it.

There were moments when Blake pushed me even further, asking me to go beyond the realm of "pretty" and affirm my own beauty on a deeper level. He would challenge me to say "I am beautiful" three to five times, urging me to embrace and celebrate my own unique radiance. Sometimes, he would even encourage me to stand in front of a mirror, looking into my own eyes as I spoke those empowering words to myself. It was an exercise in self-love and self-acceptance, a reminder that beauty resides not only in physical appearances but also in the strength, resilience, and compassion that define us as individuals.

Blake's unwavering dedication to helping me recognize my beauty was a testament to his genuine care and love. His actions went beyond the surface level, digging deep into the core of my being to build my self-confidence and foster a profound sense of self-worth. Through his encouragement and unwavering support, he became a catalyst for self-discovery and self-empowerment, forever altering my perception of myself.

To him, I was more than just pretty or beautiful—I was a reflection of the remarkable person I was becoming. He saw the potential within me and encouraged me to embrace my unique qualities and strengths. With each repetition of those affirmations, I began to believe them a little more, gradually internalizing the truth of my own beauty and finding solace in the knowledge that I was worthy of love and admiration.

Halloween weekend arrived, marking one of the most eventful times for college parties. Given the special occasion, I decided to stay at Riv for three consecutive nights instead of my usual one night a week. During this short period, my trust in Blake had grown exponentially, surpassing any level of trust I had previously placed in someone. I found myself genuinely falling in love with him. For the first time, I understood what my mom had meant when she said I didn't know what love was. This love was different, stronger, and unlike what I had experienced with Jack and Andrew. I felt ready to take the next step in our relationship, something I had never felt before. I trusted Blake completely, knowing that he would listen and respect my boundaries. I expressed my readiness to him.

"Annabelle, I'm ready too, but I want you to be certain. I don't want you to say it just for the sake of it. I will wait as long as you need." he reassured me.

The following week, it happened. Surprisingly, I wasn't scared or nervous. Blake made me feel comfortable and at ease. I won't delve into details for obvious reasons, but there is a funny part to this story. Barely a second after the fact, the door swung open.

Are you kidding me? He forgot to lock the door?

In rushed four drunken members of the baseball team, shouting Blake's name. Panicked, he urged them to leave.

"Get out, get out, get out," he repeated nervously.

I simply laughed it off. After all, they hadn't seen anything, and there was little else I could do in that moment. We decided to go to the vending machine, grabbed some snacks, and settled down to watch a movie until we eventually fell asleep.

The purpose of this chapter was to reiterate the fact that there is someone out there for everyone. When I was dealing with recovering from my past relationships, I didn't believe there would ever be anyone different. *Because I hadn't met someone different.* I didn't believe that someone would see my worth or treat me how I deserved. *But that was because I hadn't met anyone like that.* Just because you haven't met the person, doesn't mean they don't exist. You have to be patient. There is a cliche quote that is used way too often, but it is true; love will find you, when you are not looking for it. In the meantime, you have to work on yourself. You need to show yourself love, so that you can truly understand your worth and what you deserve.

On another note, beginning a new relationship after abusive ones can be terrifying. It feels uncertain and uncomfortable. A lot of times, we will want to avoid these people entirely. My advice to you is that if you feel the need to avoid a relationship with someone; *avoid it.* When the right person, and healthy relationship comes along, of course it will still be scary. Especially since it will be so much different than what you are used to. But, you won't feel the need to avoid this person or relationship. Listen to yourself and your body, it will always tell you when to steer clear, or move forward.

SIXTEEN

Unconditional Love

My dog Sully, who had entered my life when I was just twelve years old, held an indescribable significance within my heart. Throughout the years, he had grown alongside me, becoming an integral part of my journey. In those early days, Sully embodied a lively and playful puppy, always yearning to explore the great outdoors.

One of Sully's most endearing qualities was his unwavering adoration for people, particularly children. His gentle and affectionate nature allowed him to form an instant connection with anyone who crossed his path. Sully's eyes would gleam with delight, and his tail would wag with unmatched exuberance at the mere sight of a new face. But it wasn't just humans that captured his heart; Sully had a soft spot for the irresistible allure of juicy apples and cheeseburgers from McDonald's. Watching him devour these treats with pure bliss was a sight that always brought a smile to my face.

As life unfurled with its share of trials and tribulations, Sully proved to be a loyal and empathetic companion throughout. During moments of deep sadness, when tears streamed down my face in the solitude of my room, he would somehow sense the turmoil within me. In his own intuitive way, he would ascend the stairs, his paws gently padding against each step, until he reached my side. With an unwavering devotion, he would nuzzle his wet nose against my cheek, comforting me as if he understood the pain I was experiencing. His wet kisses would gently wipe away the salty trails that cascaded down my face, providing comfort in a way that only he could.

However, as I completed my first year of college, an unforeseen darkness began to cast its shadow over Sully's life. Existing health issues with his hips, which had always posed a challenge, seemed to intensify, causing him immense difficulty in rising from his bed. The vibrant appetite that once defined him waned, and even his beloved cheeseburgers and ice cream no longer enticed his taste buds. With every labored breath and every wheeze that escaped his weakened body, it was evident that something grave was afflicting him.

A couple of days later, my mother took Sully to the veterinarian, hoping for answers and a glimmer of hope. Our expectations were tempered, as these visits often entailed hours of waiting in the car before Sully received attention. But that day, fate seemed to steer us down an unexpected path. As they arrived, the staff, recognizing the urgency of the situation, promptly whisked Sully away to be examined. It took only a few fleeting minutes before the weight of the diagnosis crushed our spirits—Sully had cancer. I can still recall the heart-wrenching phone call my mother made.. In the midst of this devastating revelation, my father, his voice tinged with sorrow, approached my room. The tears welled up in his eyes, threatening to overflow, as he uttered those heart-wrenching words, "I have bad news, Sully has cancer, and we have to put him down." The floodgates of my emotions burst open, and a torrent of tears streamed down my face. In an instant, the world as I knew it shattered, and I was left grappling with a grief I had never anticipated.

In such a fragile moment, the internal struggle between wanting to preserve my memories of Sully untainted by the pain of this final farewell and the overwhelming desire to bid him a proper goodbye tore at my soul. Ultimately, the realization that this would be my last chance to see him, to hold him close, propelled me forward. Determined, I made the last-second decision to accompany my father to the animal hospital, bracing myself for the anguish that lay ahead.

As the car journey commenced, an eerie silence engulfed us, punctuated only by the faint hum of the engine. My mind wrestled with the impending reality, and a sense of impending loss weighed heavily upon my heart. The thought of parting ways with Sully forever gnawed at my every thought, threatening to consume me with an overwhelming sense of grief. Each passing moment, the gravity of the situation deepened, and I clung to cherished memories, hoping they would provide solace in the days to come.

When we finally arrived at the animal hospital, the sterile scent of antiseptic permeated the air, a stark contrast to the warmth and familiarity that Sully had brought to our lives. A mixture of trepidation and aching love propelled me forward, urging me to face the inevitable. Though a part of me longed to shield myself from the painful reality unfolding before me, I knew that Sully deserved my unwavering presence in his final moments. It was a gesture of gratitude, a small testament to the profound impact he had made on my life.

Stepping into that room, the atmosphere felt heavy, laden with sorrow and an undeniable sense of finality. As the veterinarian prepared to administer the medication, I braced myself, my heart torn between gratitude for the years we had shared and the anguish of losing him forever. Yet, in the midst of my own sorrow, I found solace in the fact that our entire family had come together to bid Sully farewell. With trembling hands and teary eyes, I reached out to caress his soft fur, his familiar warmth providing a semblance of comfort in that moment of heartache.

In the embrace of that solemn room, we surrounded him with love, whispering our final words of affection and gratitude into his perked ears. The weight of the decision to end his suffering was heavy, but the love we held for him eclipsed our own pain. And as the medication took effect, gently pulling him into eternal slumber, I found peace in knowing that Sully was no longer burdened by the weight of his illness.

Though the pain of losing him remains a tender scar on my heart, I carry with me the precious memories of our time together. Sully, the playful puppy who grew into an unwavering companion, forever etched himself in the tapestry of my life. In his absence, I find solace in knowing that his spirit lives on, woven into the fabric of my being, reminding me of the immeasurable joy and unwavering love that can be found in the presence of a loyal friend.

Loss is far from easy and grief can feel impossible. We all heal and grieve in different ways. I know for me, after the fact, I wanted to get out of the house. Sully was a huge dog, and it just felt so empty without him. Being at home was just a reminder as to what had happened earlier in the day. The first few days, I was in the denial stage. I knew he was gone, but it didn't feel real. Then the acceptance and sadness hit, and then the anger. It is important to know that the stages of grief can come in any order, at any time. And you can even go back and forth between stages. During this time, you need to allow yourself to feel the pain. It's not easy opening yourself up to emotions, but it is the healthiest option. Feel, write, communicate, whatever you need to do. Under no circumstances should you ever suppress your emotions. It will only elongate the pain, and it will take longer to heal.

SEVENTEEN

Beyond the Final Page

I firmly believe that everything happens for a reason. Despite the pain and hardships I endured in my past relationships with Jack and Andrew, I now realize that those experiences shaped me into the strong and resilient person I am today. Through those difficult times, I learned the importance of self-worth and the value of healthy relationships. I have come to appreciate the love and support I receive from the people in my life who truly care for me.

If I hadn't crossed paths with Evelyn or encountered the negative experiences at the treatment facility, I might not have developed such a profound passion for nursing. Those encounters ignited a fire within me, motivating me to pursue a career where I can make a positive impact on others' lives. The doubts and criticisms from those who didn't believe in me no longer hold power over me. Instead, I use their words as fuel to continuously prove them wrong and, more importantly, prove myself wrong when I doubt my own capabilities. When people try to bring you down with harsh words and doubts, use it to build you back up.

Breaking Free from the clutches of manipulation and reclaiming control over my own life was an arduous and challenging journey. However, it was an essential step toward rediscovering my self-worth and finding my voice once again. It reminded me that I deserved to be treated with love, respect, and understanding. It reinforced the notion that my feelings and needs were valid and deserving of consideration.

Through it all, I have learned to embrace the notion that the difficulties I faced were not in vain. They were stepping stones that propelled me forward, helping me grow stronger and allowing me to appreciate the beauty and joy that life has to offer. I am grateful for the lessons learned and the strength I gained, as they have shaped the person I am today and will continue to guide me on my journey of self-discovery and personal growth.

~~~~

"Hey, so I was going to text you tomorrow wishing you a Merry Christmas, But I didn't want to ruin your day (so I'll do it today). I mean I don't know if it would, but I would be bamboozled if I were you. Also, when I thought to myself why exactly am I messaging you Merry Christmas after months of no contact (even though I'm probably embarrassing myself) it's because I miss you and I still genuinely care about you and I feel bad (I look kind of dense saying that).

Now I expect absolutely nothing, I just have felt incredibly guilty these past few months, so I had to get some stuff off my chest. For starters, I was not a good boyfriend, and I realize that now. The whole reason I was competitive with you was because I was jealous of your success and too dense to acknowledge that. When I made that comment that you were "fucked up", (I'm an asshole for saying that) I was just projecting.

I realize now that you and me both had our own issues and I kept victimizing myself to preserve my own ego. I failed to communicate, which now that I look back on was quite childish and I've been working on that quite a bit. Unfortunately for me love is complicated, and I went into a relationship when I had a bunch of issues. Thought to myself, I'm doing this girl a disservice because I have issues and nothing can be fixed. That's when our last sort of situation happened, and I couldn't do it in person because I was too scared. I realized that honestly, your life would most likely be better without me because it seemed I was holding you back. The only time you started coming out of your shell was when we were separated, and it seemed I was right about at least one thing.

I also made the mistake of listening to others for everything when maybe I should have just thought for myself. I actually feel selfish for sending this message. I'm potentially ruining your good times. Most embarrassing part is I even called someone by your name the other day, and I literally have dreams about you all the time. The point of the matter is I feel guilty about my behavior, and am working to be a better guy, and I just had to get all this off my chest."

~~~~

This was a message I received from Andrew, months after we had broken up. We hadn't talked in months, and he decided to reach out randomly on Christmas Eve. Now, whoever is reading this may think this is an amazing apology and that he is being sincere. But I saw right through it. He is manipulative and narcissistic. Nothing would have changed. He was only trying to pull me back in again. But I wanted nothing to do with that part of my life anymore. And I was going to make sure I never heard from him again.

~~~~

"Hi, I wasn't going to respond to this but I think it's best that I do. I'm happy that you finally see my worth. These past few months I have done a ton of work on myself. I've never been happier. I did absolutely amazing my first semester of nursing school and made the best friends that I have ever had in my entire life. I've gained more confidence in myself than I have ever had. Before now, I was never able to feel confident because I was continuously brought down. But I have continued to show myself that I am more than enough. And those around me continue to remind me of that every day.

I also really hate to tell you this, but I have a boyfriend now. He is everything I've ever asked for and more. When I was with you I thought how you were treating me was normal. I thought that is what I deserved which is why I stayed when I should have left. But I see my worth now and I see what I deserve. I'm a really great person and it really sucks for you that you're just seeing it now."

~~~~

You may believe what I said came across a little harsh. But compared to what he put me through, this was nothing. I wanted him to truly understand that I had enough. I was done. Replying to him the way I did helped me realize truly how strong I had become. I finally knew my worth and had respect for myself. And if at any point in time, Jack decides to reach out, there is no question that I will respond in the same way.

Today, as I continue my journey of self-love and personal growth, I am increasingly aware of the importance of recognizing and appreciating my own worth. While I have made significant strides, I acknowledge that there are still areas of my personality and behavior that require attention and improvement. One particular challenge I face is expressing my feelings effectively. Often, I find myself bottling up my emotions, which can eventually lead to outbursts or moments of frustration directed at my loved ones. These instances leave me feeling remorseful and deeply sorry for the unintended impact of my actions.

I am committed to finding healthier ways to communicate and address my emotions. It is an ongoing process, but one that I am determined to conquer. Recognizing the need for change, I have discovered a valuable tool that aids me in building self-confidence and emotional expression—an alter ego. Creating an alter ego for myself has proven to be surprisingly helpful in becoming the best version of who I can be.

When confronted with moments of temptation, laziness, or negative thoughts, I now pause and ask myself a pivotal question: "Would the highest-version of myself engage in such behavior?" This simple inquiry serves as a guiding principle, enabling me to make choices that align with my aspirations and long-term success. If the answer is a resounding "no," I consciously choose to defy my initial inclinations and opt for actions that are more aligned with my goals and values.

For instance, when the desire to call out of work or skip a class arises, I remind myself that the best version of me would prioritize responsibility and dedication. Understanding that success and self-improvement require effort and discipline,

I strive to make choices that reflect these values, even when they may seem challenging or inconvenient in the moment.

By harnessing the power of my alter ego, I am gradually building the confidence and self-assurance needed to navigate life's challenges more effectively. While I am still a work in progress, I am grateful for the lessons I have learned and the growth I have experienced thus far. Each day presents an opportunity to nurture and cultivate the best version of myself, and I am committed to embracing that journey wholeheartedly.

EIGHTEEN

To the Readers...

If you have ever traversed a similar path, weathered through trials that inflicted deep wounds upon your being, or experienced a pain that seemed insurmountable, allow me to offer this book as a sanctuary, a place to find healing. It may not manifest immediately, for healing is a gradual process that unfolds in its own time. Yet, with each passing day, a sliver of light pierces through the darkness, illuminating the way toward a brighter tomorrow.

In moments of introspection, I implore you to stand before a mirror, gazing deeply into your own eyes, and utter those transformative words: "You are beautiful." As the words reverberate through the chambers of your heart, allow them to transcend the superficial and embrace the essence of your being. Embrace yourself wholeheartedly, wrapping your arms around your vulnerable self in a gesture of self-compassion. And as you hold yourself, allow the declaration to resound: "I love you." For within the depths of self-love lies a journey that stretches across a lifetime, an ongoing relationship that demands nurturing and care.

Banish the echoes of negativity that may linger within the recesses of your mind. Never allow the poison of self-doubt to taint your perception of the remarkable individual you are. If you would not utter those disparaging words to the person you hold dearest in your heart, then let them never escape your lips in reference to yourself. Embrace the power of self-affirmation, for your worth transcends the boundaries of external validation. With each syllable that cascades from your tongue, carve a path of self-acceptance and grace, paving the way for a kinder, gentler inner dialogue.

As you embark upon this profound journey of self-love, know that you are not alone. Reach out to those who have walked similar paths, finding solace in their stories, and drawing strength from their resilience. Share your own experiences, offering comfort to others who may be grappling with their own battles. In the tapestry of shared vulnerability, you will discover the interconnectedness of human experience and the power of collective healing.

And remember, dear reader, that healing is a nuanced and intricate tapestry, woven thread by thread, moment by moment. There will be setbacks and moments of doubt, but within the recesses of your heart lies an unwavering spirit, ready to rise and carry you through. Embrace this book as a beacon of hope, a gentle reminder that amidst the turbulence of life, there is always a glimmer of light, guiding you towards a future illuminated by love, acceptance, and the resounding beauty of your own being.

Made in the USA
Las Vegas, NV
09 January 2024

84134740R00090